A **CELEBRATE RECOVERY**® RESOURCE

John Baker
Johnny Baker

WITH RICK LAWRENCE

the Landing™

CelebrateRecovery® for Students

LEADER GUIDE 3

Pastor John Baker is the founder of Celebrate Recovery®, a ministry born out of the heart of Saddleback Church in 1991. Since then more than 11,000 individuals have gone through this Christ-centered recovery program at Saddleback. The Celebrate Recovery® program is now used in thousands of churches worldwide. Over 700,000 people have completed the program.

John is a nationally known speaker and trainer who helps churches start Celebrate Recovery® ministries. In addition to writing the *Celebrate Recovery Curriculum*, he's the general editor of the *Celebrate Recovery Bible*. John's most recent book is *Life's Healing Choices*. Since the beginning of Celebrate Recovery®, Pastor John has attempted to reach out to children in hurting homes. He's the co-author of *Celebration Station*™, Celebrate Recovery®'s program for children, and now the co-author of *The Landing*™. He's very excited about teenagers having a curriculum of their own.

John and his wife, Cheryl, have been married four decades and have served together in Celebrate Recovery® since 1991. They have two adult children, Laura and Johnny. Laura and Brian were recently married, and Johnny and his wife, Jeni, are the proud parents of John and Cheryl's three grandchildren, Maggie, Chloe, and Jimmy.

Johnny Baker has been on staff at Celebrate Recovery® since 2004 and has been the director of Celebrate Recovery® at Saddleback Church since 2007. As an adult child of an alcoholic who chose to become an alcoholic himself, Johnny is passionate about breaking the cycle of dysfunction in his family and helping other families find the tools that lead to healing and openness. Not only has he seen Celebrate Recovery® work in the lives of his parents and countless others, he has seen it work in his own life as well. He knows that because of Jesus Christ, and by continuing to stay active in Celebrate Recovery®, his children—Maggie, Chloe, and Jimmy—will never see him drink. Johnny is a nationally recognized speaker and teacher of Celebrate Recovery®, a co-author of *Celebration Station,* and an associate editor of the *Celebrate Recovery Bible*.

Rick Lawrence has been editor of GROUP Magazine for over 20 years. GROUP is the world's most widely read resource for Christian youth leaders. In his role as "Youth Ministry Champion" at Group Publishing, he leads the organization's expeditionary efforts to challenge, encourage, and equip youth pastors.

Rick has authored hundreds of magazine articles and is the author, co-author, or editor of 31 books including *Youth Ministry in the 21st Century*, *Jesus-Centered Youth Ministry*, *In Pursuit of Jesus*, and *Ten Tough Things*—all published by Group Publishing. He's a consultant to national research organizations and a frequent conference and workshop speaker.

He's married to Beverly Rose and has a 12-year-old daughter named Lucy Rose and a 7-year-old daughter named Emma Grace.

I'd like to dedicate The Landing to my wife Cheryl—without her dedication and perseverance, this project would never have happened. And to the thousands and thousands of kids who hope to find the answer to their hurts before they become hang-ups and habits.

- John Baker

I would like to dedicate The Landing to my wife Jeni, and our three kids, Maggie, Chloe, and Jimmy. I'd also like to thank Eddie, Doug, Ted, Habib, and many others who were there for me as youth workers. Your investments of time, love, and listening were instrumental in giving me a strong base of faith. Thanks for teaching me about Jesus both in your example and by your words.

- Johnny Baker

To my dear, dear daughters Lucy Rose and Emma Grace—I already see the healing love of Jesus "covering the multitude of sins" that you've had to bear in your lives, and your passion for giving grace to others inspires and challenges me.

- Rick Lawrence

THE LANDING™
A CELEBRATE RECOVERY® RESOURCE
LEADER GUIDE 3
Copyright © 2010 Group Publishing, Inc.

group.com
simplyyouthministry.com

Credits
Authors: John Baker, Johnny Baker, with Rick Lawrence
Executive Developer: Nadim Najm
Chief Creative Officer: Joani Schultz
Editor: Cheryl Baker
Copy Editor: Rob Cunningham
Cover Art and Production: Veronica Lucas
Production Manager: DeAnne Lear

ISBN 978-0-7644-6447-8

10 9 8 7 6 5 4 3 2 1   18 17 16 15 14 13 12 11 10

Printed in Canada.

TABLE OF CONTENTS

INTRODUCTION

Welcome to a grand adventure—an exciting and surprising and life-changing journey, in partnership with God. The Landing is a unique experience in at least a couple of ways.

First, it's structured as an ongoing 52-week program—based on the beatitudes where Jesus laid out principles for happiness in the sermon on the mount—for teenagers who are struggling to live their lives in a healthy, God-honoring way. Maybe they come from a dysfunctional home or have faced crises in their life. Maybe they simply need help developing patterns of wise choices, or they wrestle with an addiction of some kind. Whatever their life story, they know they need something more than a typical Sunday school class or youth group meeting. Or maybe they don't know this, but the people who love them do. The Landing is a safe, healing place where teenagers can live a freer, healthier, and more God-centered life.

Second, The Landing is not a lecture-style resource. It's designed to get teenagers talking about and exploring new ways of thinking and doing. They won't just be listening to someone speak—instead, they'll be talking to each other and to your leaders in a fully engaging environment that includes simple experiences that will help them "own" what they're learning. In most classes or small group studies, the leader controls pretty much everything about the direction of the lesson, and the teenagers just follow along. With The Landing, the leader provides strong leadership and overarching direction, and encourages the students to participate and engage in the discussion. This style of teaching helps everyone feel the satisfaction of playing a key role in the journey.

We believe that true transformation comes when you get closer to Jesus. We feel so strongly about this, we're going to write that sentence again:

We believe that true transformation comes when you get closer to Jesus.

The aim of The Landing is to help hurting teenagers get closer to Jesus as they learn key principles during a journey toward a better life—to move their focus on Jesus from the fringes of daily life to the bull's-eye of everyday life.

Finally, we want to remind you that you're about to partner with God to change the life trajectory of the people who participate in The Landing. This really will happen. People will get closer to Jesus, and they will learn about their hurts, hang-ups, and habits that have derailed them. And many of them will be changed by this experience forever. Thanks for having the courage and the determination to be a part of the nuclear moments that are about to take place. Along with the participants in the study, you'll not only end up worshiping Jesus at a deeper level, you'll also give people a pathway to freedom in their lives.

BOOT CAMP FOR LEADING THE LANDING

This yearlong experience probably differs from most studies you've led. Even if that's not the case, we've learned some vital insights over the years for leading study times that involve a lot of interactions, debriefing, and feedback. Instead of a lecture or fill-in-the-blank style—strategies that have questionable long-term impact on teenagers—we use music, video, high-octane discussions, and experiences to get at the core truths we're learning. This is a really fun, amazing way to lead people into deeper learning.

Let's explore what makes this series different and what you can expect as the leader.

THE LEADER'S ROLE

In a typical small group or youth group study, a leader talks almost the entire time. Sometimes, a couple of discussion questions get tossed out, but they're often a side dish to the real meat of the study.

In The Landing, the leader talks, but the participants talk, too. A lot. If you're leading this series, you'll feel more like a ringmaster than a lecturer. You'll offer strong leadership in a context where many people participate and add to the content of the study.

Allow us to explain why that's such a great thing.
First, research shows that teenagers learn best by doing. In fact, the people who learn the most in any class are

the teachers—because they first need to ingest what they're teaching before they teach it. So what happens when teenagers get immersed in experiences and talk to each other (and you) about what they're learning while they're learning it? Well, real learning takes place.

If you're a curious person who likes good conversation and who knows how to ask follow-up questions, you'll thrive in this learning environment. If you don't think you have any of these qualities, don't worry. We've crafted instructions for these sessions in a way that allows anyone to lead them. You simply need to see your role as a strong leader who has a lot to offer, but who wants to hear the experiences and opinions of others as well.

Of course, the most important aspect of leading this study is to let it transform you first. If you've experienced Celebrate Recovery® firsthand—this content is based on that dynamic resource—you know the life-changing power that this material has. If you haven't been through Celebrate Recovery®, allow this material to transform you as you prepare to teach it to students. As you prepare to lead, you need to pursue the questions and insights first. In essence, that's what being a leader means—going first. Preparation, prayer, and planning are essential. In these lessons, the leader provides important insights. Right now, these insights are all in our voice. You could say them verbatim, just as we've written them for you. But of course, you can filter everything through who you are. You do want to make sure to understand and own these insights—by the time you lead each lesson, you'll have explored it for yourself first and let it impact you. Throughout the lessons, we've placed the words you need to say in bold preceded by the words SAY or ASK. This allows them to stand out, and you can easily scan for what you need to say.

One more important role for you, the leader, is to help teenagers celebrate and enjoy the changes God is making in their lives as they progress through this material. The subject matter can feel heavy at times so you'll need to create an environment that allows students to feel safe, and at the same time celebrate the better choices they will be making and the victory they are finding in Jesus.

There are a few key things you can do to make the group safe for everyone. As you prepare for your lessons, ask God to point out anything you can share from your experience. Students will gain so much from your willingness to be open and honest. In fact, you may find that in order to get the discussion started you may want to share first. We've included some guidelines, which will be discussed later in the section titled Group Guidelines, that will help you and your students in answering the small group questions.

Next, as this is an ongoing 52-week program that does not close or require sign-ups, you may have some students that begin attending after you've already completed several of the lessons. It is important that these students feel safe and included here in The

Landing as well. You may want to designate some leaders or more mature students to come alongside the newcomers to help them along. In addition, you may decide to modify some of the questions to suit a younger audience, such as junior high students.

THE STUDENT JOURNAL

Each student in your class will need a Student Journal. These Student Journals are an integral part of the experience for your teenagers. The journals have material in them that complements the lessons they're going through without duplicating content. It's reading that will really help teenagers consider, process, and deepen what they're learning. Each Student Journal segment ends with a series of questions that are tied to the questions they discussed in their small groups. The journals also serve as a notebook for each participant. We've included lots of room for taking notes; keeping meaningful reminders, quotes, or Scripture references from the lessons; writing personal insights; and answering questions. Encourage participants to use the journals regularly.

These journals are intended for your students' eyes only. They should be encouraged to keep these journals in a safe place. Knowing that neither you, nor anyone else, will be reading these journals will allow the students to freely express themselves and write things they may not yet feel comfortable sharing in a group setting. Working through a journal yourself will help you better understand what your teenagers may be feeling throughout this journey.

MILESTONE MARKERS

We have provided key tags as a way to celebrate each teenager's journey through this program. These key tags are designed to celebrate significant milestones in your teenagers' participation in The Landing—Day 1, Week 2, Month 1, Month 2, Month 3, Month 6, Month 9, and Year 1. All of these tags are available at group.com or simplyyouthministry.com.

These key tags are a great visual reminder for your students to celebrate the journey and to keep focused on the changes they are making. After Closing Time, right before Connect Time, while they are still gathered together, distribute the key chains by asking the students, "Who is here for the first time?" Then proceed through the rest of the marker lengths.

WORSHIP TIME

Nearly every lesson features a Worship Time near the start of your gathering. Usually there's an activity or a conversation that precedes a time of singing some favorite worship songs or listening to songs on a CD or from your MP3 player. If you have a worship band comprised of teenagers this can be an opportunity for them to participate and lead. Or you may have a leader who plays an instrument who could lead during this time.

Sometimes we suggest playing soft and unobtrusive instrumental music as a background during discussion or experience times as well.

VIDEOS

Included in your kit are 4 DVDs (corresponding with each Leader Guide) with video clips for one of the two lessons under every topic. The instructions are easy to follow, and the video clip always precedes your small group time, which features discussion of the clip.

Be sure to preview, cue up the clips, set the volume, and test your electronics before people arrive for the session. If you're fiddling with equipment while people arrive, you basically greet them with your backside. At best, this means you're distracted as you talk with them.

EXPERIENCES

Many of the sessions in this series include experiences that participants will do and you'll then "debrief." By "experiences," we mean activities that encourage everyone to participate. These might be fun, meditative, or mildly uncomfortable. But the goal is to lead people into activities where they feel fully engaged.

"Debriefing" is just another way of saying that you will artfully engage participants with good initial questions about the experience, followed by good follow-up questions. You help the people in your group build bridges from unforgettable experiences to unforgettable truths. When you succeed, you can truly say two things: You've "taught," and the participants have "learned."

These experiences aren't just fringe illustrations or funky gimmicks. Research shows that students learn more deeply through direct experiences than any other teaching approach. You might be tempted to think lightly of these experiences, or diminish them, or cut them out if you're pressed for time. **But resist that temptation!** We know not just from research but from personal experience teaching this way, that good experiences—debriefed well by a leader—hold unmatched power to capture and change people.

We urge you to pay close attention to the details of these experiences so you can easily give instructions to participants. Preparation and planning are essential. We provide clear and specific direction on how to set up, lead, and debrief these experiences. A leader can ruin a great experience by leaving out a crucial principle, giving fuzzy directions, or not grasping the makeup of the experience itself. Even more, you'll torpedo a powerful experience if you "hedge your bets" by apologizing for or diminishing an experience in your setup for it. If you doubt that people will get much out of the experience, suspend your disbelief and just decide to believe people will do what you ask them to do. We can tell you, they will. And they'll remember the experiences years from now. However, do not be discouraged if a student chooses to not participate at first in these experiences. Your confidence that a student will eventually participate in a safe environment is crucial.

We'll talk a little more about what to cut and not cut from each session if, for some reason, time is tight. But our general rule of thumb is never cut an experience.

Instead, cut down on what you say. As much as we want to just tell people what we think they should know, a good experience will teach people a lesson they'll never forget. Keep in mind that the experiences in this journey aren't just "illustrations" or "object lessons"—they're the very meat of the study. So, more than any other aspect of this series, make sure you understand and are ready to lead the experiences.

SUPPLIES

Because the lessons contain hands-on, interactive experiences, you'll need to gather supplies before each week's meeting. Don't wait until the last minute to look at the list of items you'll need—preparation and planning are essential. We've done our best to recommend items that can be found in a typical youth room or church facility. Encourage other leaders to pitch in and help bring or acquire supplies, especially if you don't have a budget for these supplies. Whenever possible, don't buy—just bring or borrow. If you have a particularly large group of teenagers going through The Landing, you may want to pick and choose which experiences you do with everyone and perhaps leave a couple of experiences as demonstrations with a few volunteers.

In some cases, we've offered suggestions on alternative supplies for activities. These recommendations can help you save money or time in gathering supplies. Throughout this curriculum, you're welcome to substitute supplies that reduce expenses or time but continue to give teenagers a hands-on, interactive learning experience.

Here are a few notes on frequently needed supplies:

» **Paper:** Keep a lot of this handy. We ask students to write their thoughts or answer questions a lot. Teenagers can use their copies of the Student Journal, but for the ones who don't have or forget to bring their copies, keep a healthy supply of paper.

» **3X5 cards:** You'll use these a LOT! We encourage you to purchase them in large quantities before starting The Landing.

» **Pens and pencils:** Your teenagers will do a lot of writing, and we generally assume that most young people don't carry pens and pencils with them to church or small group gatherings. Keep this supply well stocked.

» **TV/DVD player:** As mentioned earlier, this kit includes a DVD with a video clip for one of the two lessons under every topic. If you have a projector system in your meeting room, go ahead and use it—don't feel constrained to use a TV.

» **Bibles:** In many of the lessons you'll be asking for students to read verses from the Bible. While some of your students may bring their own Bibles with them, and you may want to encourage them to do so, it's a good idea to have a few extra Bibles on hand. You don't have to buy any special Bible for this, just bring any Bibles you have and ask the other adult leaders to do the same. We've used a variety of Bible translations in this curriculum, but you'll see that the New International Version is most prevalent. If your youth ministry or congregation has a preferred translation, you're welcome to use it throughout your lessons.

» We've included a CD-ROM in this kit. It's full of handouts that you can use in The Landing, including small group questions, handouts for students, and **AN IMPORTANT NOTE FOR ALL LEADERS TO READ AND UNDERSTAND.** Look through the CD-ROM's contents as you're preparing for the first lesson to gain a sense of all the tools you'll find there.

DISCUSSIONS

At the heart of this series, you'll need to make a commitment to spark great discussions. As with any great discussion, you won't always be sure which way a conversation will go. You might be tempted to impose your will or your agenda on every discussion, but (for the most part) it's good to resist that temptation. Your goal should be to get every person contributing to the life and content of the sessions.

Sometimes teenagers want to follow rabbit trails— directions that stray from your plan and threaten to hijack the carefully crafted teaching thread. Often, it's OK to follow rabbit trails—as long as the trail leads toward the overarching goal of the lesson. Occasionally, a participant might take over and force the study in a different, and potentially unsafe, direction. When you sense you're getting bogged down in an unhelpful rabbit trail, stop walking down it and return to the main path.

Sometimes a student will give an answer that is confusing or irrelevant. You'll want to try hard not to place value judgments on how people answer.

The goal behind all this strategy is to make your group a safe and inviting place for people to add their voice to the conversation. Throughout The Landing, you'll switch between many kinds of interactions: partners, trios, small group, and whole-group discussions. If you believe a partner- or trio-focused discussion topic would work better for your teenagers in a larger group, then use it in that setting. The primary purpose for the variety of group sizes is to encourage everyone to participate and speak. Not all teenagers will engage as actively in the larger groups, but they'll be more willing to answer and share their views with just one or two peers.

Each lesson's small group time includes an opportunity for you to bring other safe, mature adult leaders into the journey with your teenagers. We've labeled these individuals as "conversation leaders," and their role is to facilitate that part of the lesson. We encourage you to provide these leaders with their questions in advance. If you find that you don't have enough adult leaders to serve in this role, empower your teenagers to ask the questions.

WHAT TO CUT...AND NOT

Because of the learning approach we use in this series, you might need to cut part of a session because of time. That's OK, because coverage isn't the goal of these studies. Instead, focus on deeper learning and transformation. You can feel OK about occasionally letting a conversation go on a little longer if needed. We've designed these lessons to last two hours from start to finish.

A few general guidelines about cutting stuff: Aim to cut from the middle of the session if you're tight on time, rather than the beginning or the end. Never cut an experience in favor of leader-talk. If you must choose between participants discovering a truth in discussion with others and you simply telling them the truth, opt for option A. Let others own what they're learning. You might be tempted to cut discussions short for the sake of time. If you do, you'll have a lot of frustrated people on your hands—people who simply don't have enough time to talk about the great question you asked them to pursue. These frustrated people then have a hurdle to overcome if they're going to return to the study the next week. So, cut and condense what you have to say in favor of retaining what others have to say. Don't worry, you'll still have many opportunities to guide, influence, and frame the discussions.

SMALL GROUP DYNAMICS

One of the most important parts of The Landing is the small group time. It is imperative that these groups are safe! Students will be opening up about their lives and answering questions that require personal and thoughtful answers. For this reason, there are two main factors to keep in mind when splitting your large group into small groups. First, all of the small groups in The Landing must be gender based. Boys with boys and a male leader, and girls with girls and a female leader. No exceptions. Also, as The Landing is a place for junior high as well as senior high students, you may have a wide range of ages each week. If possible, try to have the small groups be as close in age as possible, keeping in mind to always keep them gender specific. As we mentioned earlier, at different points of the lessons your students will be in groups of either pairs or trios. During these times allow students to partner with whomever they feel most comfortable.

SMALL GROUP GUIDELINES

To make sure The Landing is a safe place for students — where they can share their hurts, hang-ups, and habits — we've included five important guidelines (pp. 17-18). These guidelines are simple and straight forward, but we know they may be new to you. These guidelines are a part of every Celebrate Recovery® resource, including Celebration Station and now, here, with The Landing. By following and modeling these guidelines, and ensuring that the students in your discussion groups do as well, you'll be making The Landing a place where they can share honestly and openly. These five guidelines are integral to the success of these kinds of discussion groups.

Students need a place where they can share and not feel judged. We've done our best to make sure there aren't any questions that have "right" and "wrong" answers. The questions are designed to get students thinking and sharing. As a conversation leader you may feel from time to time the urge to shape a student's answer. Resist that temptation! Remember that these guidelines aren't just for the students, but they're for you too.

For example, Guideline 2 states, "Please avoid all cross talk." Here are some examples of cross talk:

» Two people having a discussion that excludes the rest of the group
» Agreeing or disagreeing with someone's sharing
» Asking a question about something shared

Cross talk makes a group unsafe. Students may be opening up about events and emotions for the first time ever. If they are told they should not feel a certain way, the group is no longer safe for them. If they are challenged or questioned, even just to clarify, the group may no longer feel safe for them.

As the leader you will have to model and even enforce these guidelines. When students see that each discussion will be held with these guidelines in mind, and that you follow them, too, their sharing will be deeper because they feel safe.

SMALL GROUP GUIDELINES

1. FOCUS ON YOUR OWN THOUGHTS AND FEELINGS WHEN SHARING WITH THE GROUP.

We want to be sure everyone has time to share, so please limit your sharing to three to five minutes. If you focus on your own thoughts and feelings, you're less likely to "wander" and discuss unrelated topics. As the group leader, I may let you know when you've shared for too long, but if you focus on what matters most, you'll likely stay within the time boundaries.

2. PLEASE AVOID ALL CROSS TALK.

We want each person to be free to express feelings and thoughts without interruptions. Here are some examples of "cross talk." Two individuals engage in conversation while excluding everyone else. A group member interrupts or inappropriately laughs when another person shares. Or a group member says, "I can relate to you because..." or "I can't relate to you because...." Please be respectful toward the other members of our group, because I know you want everyone to be respectful when it's your turn to share.

3. WE ARE HERE TO SUPPORT ONE ANOTHER.

Sometimes in our group settings, we hear about other people's challenges, and we want to offer solutions to fix their problems. We may have the right intention, and we may want to share the wisdom we're gaining from being in this awesome program. But the other person may not be ready or want to hear or understand. You will protect each other by simply supporting one another and not trying to "fix" one another.

4. VALUE AND PROTECT ANONYMITY AND CONFIDENTIALITY.

It hurts to discover that information someone has shared here is being discussed outside of the small group time. Some of us struggle with trust issues because we've been hurt by other people. We all need to know that this is a safe place to share. What is shared in our group stays in our group. The only exception is if someone threatens to injure himself/herself or others.

5. AVOID OFFENSIVE LANGUAGE; IT HAS NO PLACE IN A CHRIST-CENTERED GROUP.

I'd encourage everyone in this group to follow this biblical thought, found in Ephesians 4:29—*Don't use foul or abusive language. Let everything you say be good and helpful, so that your words will be an encouragement to those who hear them.*

READY

lesson twenty-eight

PRINCIPLE 5:

Voluntarily submit to every change God wants to make in my life and humbly ask him to remove my character defects.

SCRIPTURAL TRUTHS:

"Happy are those whose greatest desire is to do what God requires" (Matthew 5:6 GNT).

"Humble yourselves before the Lord, and he will lift you up" (James 4:10 NIV).

SCHEDULE

- ⁞⁞ **CONNECT TIME** (15 minutes)
- ♫ **WORSHIP** (15 minutes)
- 📖 **TEACHING TIME** (40 minutes)
- 👥 **SMALL GROUPS** (30 minutes)
- 🕐 **CLOSING** (5 minutes)
- ⁞⁞ **CONNECT TIME** (15 minutes)

SUPPLIES NEEDED

» CD player (optional)
» CD with worship music (optional)
» Paper
» Pens and pencils
» Trash can
» Several pieces of rope, each about 1 foot long (you could substitute with towels, jackets, or T-shirts)—you want enough so each student in the group can be paired with a partner

PREPARATION

» Pray for your teenagers and your meeting
» Review this lesson
» Gather supplies
» Select songs for the Worship Time

⋮ CONNECT TIME

SUPPLIES: Several pieces of rope, each about 1 foot long (you could substitute with towels, jackets, or T-shirts).

Warmly welcome everyone to the group.

Have students get in pairs. Give each pair a piece of rope (or use towel, jackets, or T-shirts). Have each student grab an end of the item. The person in each pair whose birthday is closest to today is person one; the other is person two. Explain that person one's job is to pull person two across the room by pulling on the item. Person two will attempt to keep from moving at all. Then have partners switch roles.

ASK:

» How difficult was it to pull someone behind you?
» Who got frustrated with this exercise? Why did you experience frustration?
» Did anyone get so frustrated that you decided to let go of the item? What happened when you let go?

♫ WORSHIP

SAY: I'd like us to worship God for what he's done for us. If you've been coming for a while now, you've undoubtedly seen how God led us out of our hurts, hang-ups, and habits and into a new life. If this is your first time here, I'd like to encourage you. I may not know what's going on in your life, but God does. So, in this time of worship, before we sing together, I'd like you to take a moment and think about one thing that God has done for you. Maybe God has helped you make a broken relationship right, or at least better. Maybe he's helped you avoid people that have hurt you or that pressure you to do the wrong thing. If you can't think of anything, thank God for that breath you just took, or for the steady beating of your heart. Then, with your eyes still closed, say "thank you." You can do this silently, or if you feel comfortable you can say it out loud.

Then lead kids in three familiar worship songs. If you have a youth band, invite the group to lead your teenagers in worship. Otherwise, play the songs from a CD and encourage kids to sing along—or simply play the music as everyone sits and thinks about the words of the songs.

Then have everyone read aloud, together, this week's beatitude: *"Happy are those whose greatest desire is to do what God requires"* (Matthew 5:6 GNT).

 **TEACHING TIME**

SUPPLIES: Paper, pens or pencils, and a trash can.

SAY: First, before we get started, let's take a look at where we've been so far. If you are ready to move on to Principle 5, you have done a lot of work—some of it was really hard! You faced some of the hurts, hang-ups, and habits in your life and got real about what's wrong and what's right in your life. You started to believe that God has the power to help you change, and in Principle 3, you gave your life to Jesus. Then came Principle 4. You took a good, thorough look at your life—the good and the not-so-good—and came clean about it. Wow. Seriously, let's stop for a second and just think about all that you've done, with God's help.

Here's the deal: Now is not the time to stop moving forward. You might look back and think, "Well, that's pretty good. I think I'll stop here." Please don't! You are at the part of this journey when you are READY to see God do amazing things.

To summarize what we're getting ready to do—we're ready to let go. Do you remember that scene in *Star Wars* when Luke is getting ready to blow up the Death Star? What does Obi-Wan Kenobi tell him? That's right, he says, "Let go, Luke!" I want you to imagine that God is telling you, personally, "It's time to let go."

If you have your journals, open them up to your Inventory lists. Find something on that list that you feel God is telling you it's time to let go of.

If you don't have an Inventory list, that's OK; take a second to think about your life and ask God to show you anything you've been holding on to. Ask him if there is anything that's getting in the way of him making you the person he designed you to be.

ASK:
» Why is it so hard to let go of things?
» What would make it easier?

Read 1 Peter 5:7.

ASK:

» What does that verse say to you about letting go?

Have the students each grab a piece of paper. Ask them to spread out where they have some room to write without anyone looking over their shoulder.

SAY: On that piece of paper, I'd like you to write down one thing you would love to let go of. Maybe it's a bad habit that you know life would be better without. Maybe it's a group of friends that encourage you to do things you know are wrong. Maybe it's a bad temper or a hurt feeling you've been holding on to. Write that down now. (Pause) Now, I want you to crumple that paper up.

After the students have done this, have them sit in a circle with a trash can in the middle. Make the circle as big as possible so everyone can sit a good distance away from the trash can.

SAY: When we find things in our lives we are ready to let go of, the best thing to do is well, let go. So, let's all take our papers and try to throw them away, from where we're sitting, as if we were shooting at a basketball hoop. And if you don't make your first shot, try again—and keep trying until you make a basket.

ASK:

> » How did that feel to take your paper and throw it away like that?
> » Is it that easy in real life? Why or why not?
> » In Matthew 19:26, Jesus tells us that on our own power some things are impossible, "but with God all things are possible." What does that tell you about letting go?

SMALL GROUPS

Prior to beginning your small group, read the Small Group Guidelines on pp. 17-18 with your teenagers. Remember, as a leader you are to model these guidelines for your group as you lead the discussion.

Break your larger group into small groups of three or more, with a conversation leader in each one. To prime the pump for discussion, have the leaders begin the small group time by telling about a time (using their discretion) when they gave permission to the Holy Spirit to work in them—ask them to describe, specifically, what they did to open themselves to the Spirit. Then have groups each discuss these questions (available on the CD-ROM):

Remember, as the leader, you may want to model some of these answers for your group by sharing from your own experience.

ASK:

» Is there anything in your life you feel like God is telling you to let go of? If you feel comfortable, would you like to share what it is?

» Is there anything in your life you're afraid to let go of?

» Is there anything you've tried to let go of in the past, but it keeps coming back?

» What's one thing you've learned today that may help you let go of it for good?

» Have you been successful in letting something go? How did that make you feel?

The leader of the group should close this time with a prayer that offers God thanks for the work of the Holy Spirit in our lives.

 **CLOSING**

Don't forget to remind your students to spend time with their journals this week, reflecting on what God is teaching them during this journey.

Close by reading the Serenity Prayer together (available on p. 3 of their Student Journal). Keep in mind, some teenagers may not want to read aloud with the rest of the group. That's OK; encourage them to focus on the words being shared.

God, grant me the serenity
to accept the things I cannot change,
the courage to change the things I can,
and the wisdom to know the difference.
Living one day at a time,
enjoying one moment at a time;
Accepting hardship as a pathway to peace;
Taking, as Jesus did,
this sinful world as it is;
Not as I would have it;
Trusting that you will make all things right
If I surrender to your will; So that I
may be reasonably happy in this life
and supremely happy with you forever
in the next. AMEN.

- Reinhold Niebuhr

CONNECT TIME

Serve refreshments of some kind so kids and leaders
can hang out and connect. Consider having some
healthy options for those who may use food as a way of
coping. A ping-pong table, foosball table, or even a few
board games will give teenagers an excuse to connect.

the Landing

READY

lesson twenty-nine

PRINCIPLE 5:

Voluntarily submit to every change God wants to make in my life and humbly ask him to remove my character defects.

SCRIPTURAL TRUTHS:

"Happy are those whose greatest desire is to do what God requires" (Matthew 5:6 GNT).

"Humble yourselves before the Lord, and he will lift you up" (James 4:10 NIV).

SCHEDULE

- **CONNECT TIME** (15 minutes)
- **WORSHIP** (10 minutes)
- **TEACHING TIME** (30 minutes)
- **VIDEO TIME** (10 minutes)
- **SMALL GROUPS** (35 minutes)
- **CLOSING** (5 minutes)
- **CONNECT TIME** (15 minutes)

SUPPLIES NEEDED

- » CD player (optional)
- » CD with worship music (optional)
- » TV and DVD player
- » The Landing DVD 3
- » A bag or a box
- » Six dice for every four people; you can still play the game in this lesson if you can't collect more than six dice
- » Paper
- » Pens or pencils
- » Your car keys
- » Bibles
- » Handful of everyday items that go unnoticed around the house

PREPARATION

- » Pray for your teenagers and your meeting
- » Review this lesson
- » Gather supplies
- » Select songs for the Worship Time
- » Scatter the everyday items in your meeting area

 **CONNECT TIME**

SUPPLIES: A bag or a box.

Warmly welcome everyone to the group.

Ask your teenagers to wander around your meeting room, looking for things that could represent or be considered random "clutter"—ask them to each find two things and bring them back to your group.

Ask your teenagers to form a circle. Place the items in a bag or box. One at a time, have kids kid close their eyes, reach into the bag or box, and grab one item. Before removing the item from the bag or box, have the teenager attempt to identify what this random object is. Then have the kid remove the item and see how accurate the guess was. Give every kid a chance to participate. Go around the group twice (the kids should have contributed two items each to the collection).

After your second time around the group, **SAY: Once we identify the things that are cluttering up our lives, we can get rid of them—we can ask God to clear out the junk, creating more space for him in our lives.**

♫ WORSHIP

SAY: When we offer to God the things that are cluttering up our life—stuff that's keeping us from a strong focus on our relationship with him—it's an act of worship. So right now, think of things that are cluttering up your life, that are holding you back on your journey toward a more healthy, God-centered life. (Pause) **Now let's go around our circle, with each person piling a "clutter" object in the center of the circle and silently "naming" it as something that's cluttering your life right now—but you're offering it**

to God. The object doesn't have to reflect the area of clutter in your life. For example, if partying is cluttering my life, I'd put one of my objects in the center of the circle and simply say "partying," even if the object is unrelated to partying.

After you've gone through two rounds of teenagers placing objects in the center of the circle, **SAY: The Inventory you filled you filled out a few weeks back probably helped you think of some things in your life that you need to let go of. We've just let go of something that's important to us.**

Then lead kids in three familiar worship songs. If you have a youth band, invite the group to lead your teenagers in worship. Otherwise, play the songs from a CD and encourage kids to sing along—or simply play the music as everyone sits and thinks about the words of the songs.

Then have everyone read aloud, together, this week's beatitude: *"Happy are those whose greatest desire is to do what God requires" (Matthew 5:6 GNT).*

 ## TEACHING TIME

SUPPLIES: six dice for every four people, paper, pens or pencils, your car keys, and Bibles. Collect dice from board games at home, have kids bring them in, or buy an inexpensive set from a toy store.

Form teams of four to play the dice game Farkle—you'll need six dice, a piece of paper, and a pencil for each team. The normal object of the game is to be the first to get to a designated score, such as 5,000—but for this lesson, have your teenagers play for about five minutes, then stop. If kids are familiar with this game, they may say that there are other rolls that produce a score, but we encourage you to stick to a few simple ways of scoring points, as described in these instructions (available on the CD-ROM).

SAY: Each player takes a turn rolling dice. In order not to "farkle," each roll must produce a "score." Scoring dice are set aside and contribute to the total score for that turn. A player then decides to keep his or her points or continue with the remaining dice in order to add to the total for that round. If all six dice score, the player has the option to pick up all six dice and continue accumulating points. The turn continues until a player either chooses to stop, or rolls something that doesn't score (farkle). If players farkle, they will lose all the points they have accumulated on that turn.

Here's how you keep score: rolling a 1 on a die is worth 100 points; rolling a 5 on a die is worth 50 points; and rolling three of a kind is the face-value multiplied by 100 (for example, three 2's equal 200, and three 4's equal 400—one exception is that three 1's equal 1,000 points).

If you're unable to collect enough dice to allow all your teenagers to participate in the game, run one game that everyone else can watch. Rotate a different group of kids into the game after two or three minutes.

After kids have played Farkle for five minutes or so,
ASK:
> » How does risk play into winning or losing this game?
> » In general, is it better to risk or not? Explain.
> » While you were playing, when and why did you decide to settle for what you had?

Your teenagers are likely to answer the last question in one of four ways: (1) When I'm afraid of losing what I have; (2) When I think what I have is enough or more valuable than the risk involved in trying to get more; (3) When the goal is about getting the highest score, not risking the most; or (4) When I have a lead, I take fewer chances. If kids don't offer any of these four answers, suggest them at the end of the conversation.

SAY: I never said that the object of this game was to get the highest score. What if I told you that the winner was the person with the most farkles? You assumed the goal was to get the most points. What if the goal was to see who was willing to risk the most?

ASK:
> » Think about the reasons you gave for not risking any longer in the game. How do these reasons

explain the choices we make in other parts of
our lives?
» Is taking a risk always a good thing? Explain.
» What does God think about taking risks?

After your teenagers respond, **SAY:** Let's look at a
story that Jesus tells us about what we can gain
when we risk it all for him.

Read aloud Matthew 25:14-30. Then ask one of your
teenagers to summarize the story for everyone.

ASK:

» What was the reasoning behind the two different
kinds of reactions the master had to the
servants' actions?
» Is it fair that the master gave each servant a
different amount? Why or why not?
» How do you think the master would've
responded if one of the servants put the money
to work but lost it in the process?

SAY: Here's the secret to unlocking the story: Look
at verse 14: "It will be like a man going on a journey,
who called his servants and entrusted <u>his</u> property
to them."

After kids respond, pull out your car keys and **ASK:**
» What if I let you borrow my car—would you treat
it the same as if it were yours? Why or why not?
» If I'm entrusting you with it, whose car is it?
» So who is really taking the risk in this story?

SAY: We are the servants in the story. God is the master, and he has *entrusted* us with all kinds of things: knowledge, possessions, relationships, athleticism, and even our future. These things seem like they're ours, but they're really his; he didn't have to entrust us with them. In fact, *we are his*. One day, God will return to see how we took care of these things of his—he'll want to know what you did with the gifts you've already received here in The Landing. And that's so important when we consider where we are in this journey. You've learned a lot and risked a lot already. But here comes the biggest risk so far—it's time to say to God that you're ready to make some changes, not just talk about changes. Remember, *he* is the one taking the risk. Nothing—no treasure, skill, or relationship—is ours. It's only been entrusted to us. But God has already given us the perfect example in Jesus—he took the ultimate risk, and he paid the ultimate price. God wants us to be a risk-taker like him, *for him*. It's like playing Farkle when the goal is to risk the most for our relationship with God. It's a promise—if we go all out for Jesus with everything he has entrusted us with, *we can't lose*.

Ask your teenagers to take the next risk in their journey by telling God they're ready to make changes in their life. Tell them they can talk about this next step in their small group time, after they've watched a video skit on what it looks like to tell God you're ready for change.

VIDEO TIME

Set up a DVD player and TV in your meeting area. Ahead of time, cue up the video "Don't Waste Your Life" from DVD 3 in the kit. Play the video—this one is 9:22 long.

SMALL GROUPS

Prior to beginning your small group, read through the following Small Group Guidelines with your teenagers.

1. **Focus on your own thoughts and feelings when sharing with the group.**
2. **Please avoid ALL cross talk.**
3. **We are here to support one another.**
4. **Value and protect anonymity and confidentiality.**
5. **Avoid offensive language; it has no place in a Christ-centered group.**

Remember, as a leader you are to model these guidelines for your group as you lead the discussion.

After the whole group has watched the video, split into your small groups, with a conversation leader in each one. Have your conversation leaders ask these questions (available on the CD-ROM) about the video, with the intent to draw out personal stories from the kids in the group.

Remember, as the leader, you may want to model some of these answers for your group by sharing from your own experience.

ASK:
- » As you watched the video, what impacted you the most? Explain.
- » What are some things that keep you from taking risks on this journey toward freedom?
- » Why is it relatively easy to talk about change, but hard to actually make the changes?
- » What can we do, today, to show "the master" that we're willing to take risks to make changes in our life?

At the end of this discussion, the leader should close in prayer, thanking God for cleansing us from our sins.

 **CLOSING**

Play Farkle again, in the same groups that played it during your Teaching Time. But this time encourage your teenagers to play the game with risk-taking, not accumulating points, as the goal.

After five minutes or so, **ASK:**
- » What was different about playing the game this time?
- » How did you feel as you played this time?

Close by reading the Serenity Prayer together (available on p. 3 of their Student Journal). Keep in mind, some teenagers may not want to read aloud with the rest of the group. That's OK; encourage them to focus on the words being shared.

God, grant me the serenity
to accept the things I cannot change,
the courage to change the things I can,
and the wisdom to know the difference.
Living one day at a time,
enjoying one moment at a time;
Accepting hardship as a pathway to peace;
Taking, as Jesus did,
this sinful world as it is;
Not as I would have it;
Trusting that you will make all things right
If I surrender to your will; So that I
may be reasonably happy in this life
and supremely happy with you forever
in the next. AMEN.

- Reinhold Niebuhr

Don't forget to remind your students to spend time with their journals this week, reflecting on what God is teaching them during this journey.

Serve refreshments of some kind so kids and leaders can hang out and connect. Consider having some healthy options for those who may use food as a way of coping. A ping-pong table, foosball table, or even a few board games will give teenagers an excuse to connect.

VICTORY

lesson thirty

PRINCIPLE 5:

Voluntarily submit to every change God wants to make in my life and humbly ask him to remove my character defects.

SCRIPTURAL TRUTHS:

"Happy are those whose greatest desire is to do what God requires" (Matthew 5:6 GNT).

"Humble yourselves before the Lord, and he will lift you up" (James 4:10 NIV).

"If we confess our sins, he is faithful and just and will forgive us our sins and purify us from all unrighteousness" (1 John 1:9 NIV).

SCHEDULE

- **CONNECT TIME** (15 minutes)
- ♫ **WORSHIP** (15 minutes)
- **TEACHING TIME** (40 minutes)
- **SMALL GROUPS** (30 minutes)
- **CLOSING** (5 minutes)
- **CONNECT TIME** (15 minutes)

SUPPLIES NEEDED

- » CD player (optional)
- » CD with worship music (optional)
- » 3X5 cards—one per teenager
- » Pens or pencils
- » Bibles
- » Paper
- » Cans of Pepsi and Coke; each group of three teenagers will need one can of each soda—to save money, you could purchase 2-liter bottles instead of individual cans (you also could replace "Pepsi and Coke" with "milk and orange juice" or "tea and coffee" or similar pairs of beverages)
- » Paper or plastic cups

PREPARATION

- » Pray for your teenagers and your meeting
- » Review this lesson
- » Gather supplies
- » Select songs for the Worship Time

⁘ CONNECT TIME

SUPPLIES: 3X5 cards, and pens or pencils.

Warmly welcome everyone to the group.

This is an opening "connect" activity that you're doing once every month. Have teenagers get in a circle. Give them each a 3X5 card and something to write with (if they don't already have a pen or pencil). Ask them to write one creative question on their card that's designed to discover what their friends in the group think, feel, and believe. For example: "If you were stuck somewhere, what three things would you want with you?" Or "What is one talent you have that you wish everyone knew about?"

Ask teenagers to pass the cards to you, then quickly select five question-cards based on which ones you think would be most interesting to answer. Then ask a teenager to volunteer to sit in a chair in the middle of your circle—the "Hot Seat." One by one, ask the Hot Seat person the five questions.

Encourage the remaining kids in the circle to ask at least two follow-up questions (total) after every answer from the Hot Seat person.

♫ WORSHIP

Lead kids in three familiar worship songs. If you have a youth band, invite the group to lead your teenagers in worship. Otherwise, play the songs from a CD and encourage kids to sing along—or simply play the music as everyone sits and thinks about the words of the songs.

Then have everyone read aloud, together, this week's beatitude: *"Happy are those whose greatest desire is to do what God requires"* (Matthew 5:6 GNT).

SUPPLIES: Bibles, cans of Pepsi and Coke, cups, paper, and pens or pencils. See the Supplies Needed list at the beginning of the lesson for possible variations on the "Pepsi and Coke" theme.

Have your teenagers form groups of three. Pass out cups and cans of Pepsi and Coke to each group. Tell half of the groups to build a case in support of the argument that "Pepsi is better than Coke." Assign the other half of the groups to build a case in support of the argument that "Pepsi is not better than Coke." Give groups about five minutes to taste their drinks and come up with supporting evidence for their argument. Once they've prepared their cases, read aloud this statement: "Pepsi is better than Coke." Then have groups present their case one group at a time, alternating sides.

Afterward, **ASK:**
   » **Which points did you find most compelling from the opposing side?**
   » **How much did your own personal preference for Pepsi or Coke influence your ability to defend your position? Explain.**
   » **In this activity, what did you learn about what's effective and what's not in defending "truths"?**

SAY: In Romans 1:18 through 3:20, Paul plays the role of a prosecuting attorney as he builds a convincing case that all of us have blown it. Essentially, our verdict is guilty. But now Paul puts on a new hat, beginning in Romans 3:21, where he becomes a defense attorney. He overturns our guilty verdict and argues for our innocence—not based on anything we've done, but instead, what Jesus did for us.

Next, have trios read aloud Romans 3:21-31 and work together to write a creative summary of the passage, outlining and explaining Paul's main points. Give each group a unique assignment. Have one group summarize the passage as if they were explaining it to a farmer, using farming lingo; have other groups explain the passage to a surfer, a rapper, a scientist, a child, and so on. Distribute paper or have teenagers use their Student Journals for this task; the kids should still have pens or pencils from the earlier Connect Time activity. After 10 minutes or so, gather everyone and invite groups to each share their unique explanations.

Then **SAY:** Though you've all said it different ways, we've zeroed in on the key point of Paul's defense strategy: Even though we're guilty of sin, God offered his Son Jesus as a sacrifice so that we who believe would be declared not guilty and righteous. This is the path we take to find victory over our sins—the character defects we've already listed on our inventories. We can't *argue* our way out of our own sins and defects—we must depend on Jesus' power to change us, to bring us the victory we can't produce on our own. That means we give him our permission to change us, then cooperate with the work he wants to do in us.

ASK:
» Which verse, phrase, or word in this passage means the most to you personally, and why?
» How could this passage change the way you're trying to overcome your hurts, hang-ups, and habits?

Have your teenagers each find a place in the room where they can have some space to themselves, then **SAY:** Let's close our Teaching Time by taking a look at our inventories. For the next few minutes I'd like you to focus on just one thing on your list that you'd like to find victory over—*just one thing*. Silently, do whatever you think you need to do to offer that thing up to God—to ask him to show you the path you need to walk, with his strength, to overcome that character issue.

After five minutes or so, close in prayer, thanking God for doing what we can't.

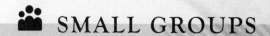

SMALL GROUPS

Prior to beginning your small group, read through the following Small Group Guidelines with your teenagers.

1. **Focus on your own thoughts and feelings when sharing with the group.**
2. **Please avoid ALL cross talk.**
3. **We are here to support one another.**
4. **Value and protect anonymity and confidentiality.**
5. **Avoid offensive language; it has no place in a Christ-centered group.**

Remember, as a leader you are to model these guidelines for your group as you lead the discussion.

Break your larger group into small groups of three or more, with a conversation leader in each one. To prime the pump for discussion, have the leaders begin the small group time by telling about a time (using their discretion) when they found victory over a character defect or a hurt, hang-up, or habit. Then have groups each discuss these questions (available on the CD-ROM).

Remember, as the leader, you may want to model some of these answers for your group by sharing from your own experience.

ASK:

» What have your past attempts to overcome your character issues or hurts, hang-ups, or habits been like?

» Paul goes to great lengths to show us that all of us, every single person, is imprisoned by sin and can't get out—why is this truth so important?

» Most of us have exhausted ourselves trying to "get better"—why is that path a hopeless one for us?

» Instead of trying hard to get better, what's something you could do every day to trust in God's power to bring you victory?

» What's the most difficult thing about trusting God to give us victory over our issues, rather than trusting ourselves to do it?

The leader of the group should close this time with a prayer that offers God thanks for the victory he's already bringing in our lives.

 **CLOSING**

Don't forget to remind your students to spend time with their journals this week, reflecting on what God is teaching them during this journey.

Close by reading the Serenity Prayer together (available on p. 3 of their Student Journal). Keep in mind, some teenagers may not want to read aloud with the rest of the group. That's OK; encourage them to focus on the words being shared.

God, grant me the serenity
to accept the things I cannot change,
the courage to change the things I can,
and the wisdom to know the difference.
Living one day at a time,
enjoying one moment at a time;
Accepting hardship as a pathway to peace;
Taking, as Jesus did,
this sinful world as it is;
Not as I would have it;
Trusting that you will make all things right
If I surrender to your will; So that I
may be reasonably happy in this life
and supremely happy with you forever
in the next. AMEN.

- Reinhold Niebuhr

 **CONNECT TIME**

Serve refreshments of some kind so kids and leaders can hang out and connect. Consider having some healthy options for those who may use food as a way of coping. A ping-pong table, foosball table, or even a few board games will give teenagers an excuse to connect.

VICTORY

lesson thirty-one

VICTORY lesson thirty-one

PRINCIPLE 5:

Voluntarily submit to every change God wants to make in my life and humbly ask him to remove my character defects.

SCRIPTURAL TRUTHS:

"Happy are those whose greatest desire is to do what God requires" (Matthew 5:6 GNT).

"Humble yourselves before the Lord, and he will lift you up" (James 4:10 NIV).

"If we confess our sins, he is faithful and just and will forgive us our sins and purify us from all unrighteousness" (1 John 1:9 NIV).

SCHEDULE

- **CONNECT TIME** (15 minutes)
- **WORSHIP** (10 minutes)
- **TEACHING TIME** (35 minutes)
- **VIDEO TIME** (5 minutes)
- **SMALL GROUPS** (35 minutes)
- **CLOSING** (5 minutes)
- **CONNECT TIME** (15 minutes)

SUPPLIES NEEDED

» CD player (optional)
» CD with worship music (optional)
» TV and DVD player
» The Landing DVD 3
» Variety of stickers that represent the interests of teenagers—you could purchase at Hobby Lobby, Michaels, or a dollar store, or through a website like orientaltrading.com (Oriental Trading Co.)
» Paper
» Scissors
» Tape
» Bibles
» Pens or pencils
» Colorful markers
» Copies of handout with "Superheroes" and "Jesus' Power" content—one per teenager (available on the CD-ROM)

PREPARATION

» Pray for your teenagers and your meeting
» Review this lesson
» Gather supplies
» Select songs for the Worship Time
» Make copies of the "Superheroes" and "Jesus' Power" handout (available on the CD-ROM)

 **CONNECT TIME**

SUPPLIES: a variety of stickers that represent the interests of teenagers, such as sports, music, movies, food, cars, and so on. Be sure to find stickers that match the gender and maturity level of your kids—high school senior guys won't enjoy the same kinds of stickers as seventh-grade girls.

Warmly welcome everyone to the group.

As your teenagers arrive at The Landing, display the stickers and ask them to each pick one that represents something they feel passionately about. Have them stick that sticker to their forehead. Then have them pair up with someone and answer these questions.

ASK:

- » What's one experience you've had related to your sticker?
- » What's one underlying reason why you're so passionate about this activity or thing?
- » How has this passion impacted your relationships with others, and even with God?

After a few minutes, gather everyone together and **SAY:** Maybe it's weird thinking about it this way, but if God had a sticker on his forehead, it would look like you—you are his passion. God loves you, can't stop thinking about you, and wants to be in close relationship with you. That's what our time here in

The Landing is all about—finding our way to the God who loves us with all his heart, leaving behind destructive patterns that hurt us.

♫ WORSHIP

SUPPLIES: paper, colorful markers, scissors, and tape.

Get your teenagers in a circle. Pile the supplies in the middle of the circle.

Tell your teenagers to create their own "sticker" that represents something about God that they're passionate about. It could be God's love, peace, mercy, strength, beauty, or forgiveness—anything about God that they feel strongly about. After they've created their sticker, they should cut it out and then put a loop of tape on the back, then stick it somewhere visible on themselves—or they could attach it to their Bible or Student Journal.

Have them find a new partner and discuss these questions.

ASK:
» What's one experience you've had with God related to the word represented on the "sticker" you created?
» What's one underlying reason why you're so passionate about this aspect of God?
» How has this passion impacted your life?

After a few minutes, gather back together and lead kids in one or two familiar worship songs. If you have a youth band, invite the group to lead your teenagers in worship. Otherwise, play the songs from a CD and encourage kids to sing along—or simply play the music as everyone sits and thinks about the words of the songs.

Then have everyone read aloud, together, this week's beatitude: *"Happy are those whose greatest desire is to do what God requires" (Matthew 5:6 GNT).*

 TEACHING TIME

SUPPLIES: Bibles, pens or pencils, and copies of the handout with the "Superheroes" and "Jesus' Power" content.

Have teenagers form trios and pass out Bibles, pens or pencils, and the handouts with the "Superheroes" and "Jesus' Power" content. Challenge kids to work with their group members to rank the superheroes from most to least powerful.

After a few minutes, have groups explain their rankings and defend their rationale.

Then **ASK:**
  » In general, why do we consider heroes more powerful than others?

Have groups work together to each write a one-sentence definition of "power" on their handouts. After a few minutes, have the trios each present their definition.

Then **SAY:** Let's explore how the idea of "power" compares to the idea of "authority." Take five minutes to search through the book of Matthew for examples of Jesus demonstrating his power and his authority—take notes whenever you find an example of either one.

After five minutes gather and ask each group to share two examples they found of Jesus' power and authority. Then read aloud John 1:1-3 and 13:3.

SAY: Jesus is God, and that means he has all the power in the universe—*all of it*. And that means his power is enough to change your life around. You may not have all you need to do the job, but he has more than enough to get the job done. And, what's more, he's told us that as his disciples we can take "authority" over the things that threaten to destroy us.

Read aloud Matthew 10:1, 8; then **ASK:**
  » What does it mean that Jesus gave his disciples "authority" over sickness, death, and demons?
  » How were they supposed to "apply" this new authority?

Have teenagers get back in their trios and work through the "Jesus' Power" content. Then gather everyone back together and ask kids to share their thoughts from questions five and six.

SAY: It isn't easy to overcome the hurts, hang-ups, and habits we've built up in our lives, but we have the power of God on our side!

Read aloud Matthew 28:18-20, then **SAY:** Jesus is with us, fueling us with his power and authority over the things that threaten us, as we live for him.

📹 VIDEO TIME

Set up a DVD player and TV in your meeting area. Ahead of time, cue up the video "Come Awake" from DVD 3 in the kit. Play the video—this one is 3:50 long.

SMALL GROUPS

Prior to beginning your small group, read through the following Small Group Guidelines with your teenagers.

1. Focus on your own thoughts and feelings when sharing with the group.
2. Please avoid ALL cross talk.
3. We are here to support one another.
4. Value and protect anonymity and confidentiality.
5. Avoid offensive language; it has no place in a Christ-centered group.

Remember, as a leader you are to model these guidelines for your group as you lead the discussion.

After the whole group has watched the video, split into your small groups, with a conversation leader in each one. Have your conversation leaders ask these questions (available on the CD-ROM) about the video, with the intent to draw out personal stories from the kids in the group.

Remember, as the leader, you may want to model some of these answers for your group by sharing from your own experience.

ASK:

» As you watched the video, what impacted you the most? Explain.

» Have you experienced victory in your life? If so, where?

» Do you think it's possible to experience victory over hard things that are out of your control?

» What does the phrase "come awake" mean to you?

At the end of this discussion, the leader should close in prayer, thanking God for cleansing us from our sins.

 CLOSING

SUPPLIES: Any remaining stickers from connect time activity.

Gather everyone back in a circle and bring out the remaining stickers from your opening Connect Time— pile them in the middle. Ask your teenagers to find a new sticker that, somehow, represents something God is helping them overcome or something that represents their journey to freedom. Encourage them to be creative—it doesn't have to connect literally to the sticker they choose. For example, if they choose a sticker of a car, they could say that God is helping them overcome an addiction to things that are supposed to make us happy.

Once everyone has chosen a sticker, go around the circle, asking volunteers to describe what their sticker represents.

Close by reading the Serenity Prayer together (available on p. 3 of their Student Journal). Keep in mind, some teenagers may not want to read aloud with the rest of the group. That's OK; encourage them to focus on the words being shared.

God, grant me the serenity
to accept the things I cannot change,
the courage to change the things I can,
and the wisdom to know the difference.
Living one day at a time,
enjoying one moment at a time;
Accepting hardship as a pathway to peace;
Taking, as Jesus did,
this sinful world as it is;
Not as I would have it;
Trusting that you will make all things right
If I surrender to your will; So that I
may be reasonably happy in this life
and supremely happy with you forever
in the next. AMEN.

- Reinhold Niebuhr

Don't forget to remind your students to spend time with their journals this week, reflecting on what God is teaching them during this journey.

Serve refreshments of some kind so kids and leaders can hang out and connect. Consider having some healthy options for those who may use food as a way of coping. A ping-pong table, foosball table, or even a few board games will give teenagers an excuse to connect.

AMENDS
lesson thirty-two

PRINCIPLE 6:

Evaluate all my relationships. Offer forgiveness to those who have hurt me and make amends for harm I've done to others, except when to do so would harm them or others.

SCRIPTURAL TRUTHS:

"Happy are the merciful" (Matthew 5:7 GNT).

"Happy are the peacemakers" (Matthew 5:9 GNT).

"Do to others as you would have them do to you" (Luke 6:31 NIV).

SCHEDULE

- ⠿ **CONNECT TIME** (15 minutes)
- ♪ **WORSHIP** (15 minutes)
- 📖 **TEACHING TIME** (40 minutes)
- 👥 **SMALL GROUPS** (30 minutes)
- ⏰ **CLOSING** (5 minutes)
- ⠿ **CONNECT TIME** (15 minutes)

SUPPLIES NEEDED

» CD player (optional)
» CD with worship music (optional)
» Pile of magazines with plenty of pictures (be careful of which magazines you choose—if you have any doubt, don't use it!)
» Different-color markers
» 3X5 cards—one per teenager
» Pens or pencils

PREPARATION

» Pray for your teenagers and your meeting
» Review this lesson
» Gather supplies
» Select songs for the Worship Time

∴ CONNECT TIME

Warmly welcome everyone to the group.

Here's an idea you'll do on occasion. Gather teenagers in a circle for this Q&A opener—the catch is they have to answer questions in the third person (meaning, they refer to themselves by name instead of using "I"). You can change the questions each time to make your opening activity fresh—we'll use this idea a handful of times throughout the year.

Use fun questions such as:

» **What ice cream flavor would you like to create?**
» **Share with us one obscure fact about yourself.**

» What's your biggest pet peeve and how does it make you feel?
» What was your favorite book when you were younger?
» What are you going to do after you graduate from high school?

Add your own questions to this list. It's funny to hear people talk about themselves this way—but this opener has the added benefit of cementing kids' names in their memory, and providing some fun stories about each other.

 WORSHIP

ASK:
» The book of Genesis in the Bible tells us how Adam and Eve made a choice that fractured their relationship with God. If you had been Adam or Eve, and you knew that you'd completely blown your relationship with God and that there was no way you could fix things on your own, what would you be feeling?
» When have you experienced that feeling before in a relationship with another person?

SAY: God knows we can't fix things on our own, so because of his great love for us, he does the fixing— God offers his only Son Jesus as the payment for our sin, to restore our blown relationship with him.

Let's worship God now for his goodness and mercy toward us.

Then lead kids in three familiar worship songs. If you have a youth band, invite the group to lead your teenagers in worship. Otherwise, play the songs from a CD and encourage kids to sing along—or simply play the music as everyone sits and thinks about the words of the songs.

Then have everyone read aloud, together, this week's beatitudes: *"Happy are the merciful"* (Matthew 5:7 GNT) and *"Happy are the peacemakers"* (Matthew 5:9 GNT).

 # TEACHING TIME

SUPPLIES: a pile of magazines with plenty of pictures, different-color markers, 3X5 cards, and pens or pencils.

SAY: In Principle 1, you faced some of the hurts, hang-ups, and habits in your life and gotten real about what's wrong and what's right in your life. In Principle 2, you started to believe that God has the power to help you change, and in Principle 3, you gave your life to Jesus. Then in Principle 4, you took a good, thorough look at your life and came clean about both the good, and the not so good. In Principle 5, you let go of some of the things keeping you back from being the person God wants you to be. In Principle 6, you'll look at your relationships, say sorry for the things you did to hurt other people, and forgive people who have hurt you. Making amends for the wrong things we've done or said involves much more than simply saying a casual "I'm sorry." Making amends involves a genuine change of heart that's sealed by action.

Somewhere in the center of your gathering, pile the different-color markers and the magazines. Ask your teenagers to each find a picture of someone or something from one of the magazines and tear out that page to work with. Once everyone has a picture to work with, SAY: Take the markers I've piled here and draw something new right over the picture you've torn out—you could draw a mountain scene over a picture of someone, or you could draw your family over a picture of a car. Whatever you do, decide on something to draw, and then draw it on top of your picture. Try to cover as much of the picture with your drawing as possible. I'll give you 10 minutes to do this.

After 10 minutes or so, ask your kids to show off their masterpieces. Then SAY: What you've done here is an example of a term used in the art world— "*pentimento*"—that refers to a painting that's been painted on top of an older finished canvas. Occasionally, as years pass, a painting will fade, exposing another painting lying underneath. Likely, the artist changed his or her mind and painted right over a previous "mistake." *Pentimento* is actually the Italian word for repentance. Sometimes we apply *pentimento* to our own lives. We see the mess we've made. We have a change of heart and want to start over fresh. We summon the courage to repent and make amends for the hurt we've caused. Only then is God able to paint a new life over our existing one. There may still be evidence there of the old you—bad choices sometimes carries consequences that are irreversible. And sometimes traces of your old self may even shine through. But for the most part, your life is now about something altogether different. It's a thing of beauty. The Master's piece.

ASK:

» What's the difference between a simple apology and true repentance?
» What typically happens when you're sorry for what you've done, but you don't do anything to make amends? Explain.
» Is it always possible to do something to make amends for the hurt you've caused? Why or why not?

Read aloud Matthew 5:23-24: *"Therefore, if you are offering your gift at the altar and there remember that your brother has something against you, leave your gift there in front of the altar. First go and be reconciled to your brother; then come and offer your gift."*

ASK

» Can you "be reconciled" to another person if that person doesn't want to be reconciled, maybe because he or she isn't over the hurt? Why or why not?

» How can you make amends for what you've
done, no matter how the people you've hurt feel?

Give your teenagers each a 3X5 card and a pen or
pencil. On one side have them each write a heartfelt
apology to God for things they've done that have hurt
their relationship with him. On the other side, have them
think of a hurt they've caused someone and come up
with an idea for how they could make amends for that
hurt. Tell them to hold on to that card as they move to
their small group.

 **SMALL GROUPS**

Prior to beginning your small group, read through the
following Small Group Guidelines with your teenagers.

1. Focus on your own thoughts and feelings when
   sharing with the group.
2. Please avoid ALL cross talk.
3. We are here to support one another.
4. Value and protect anonymity and confidentiality.
5. Avoid offensive language; it has no place in a
   Christ-centered group.

Remember, as a leader you are to model these
guidelines for your group as you lead the discussion.

Break your larger group into small groups of three or
more, with a conversation leader in each one. To prime

the pump for discussion, have the leaders begin the small group time by telling about a time (using their discretion) when they forgave someone, or received forgiveness from someone. Then have groups each discuss these questions (available on the CD-ROM).

Remember, as the leader, you may want to model some of these answers for your group by sharing from your own experience.

ASK:

> » What's your idea for making amends in your life? (If someone feels comfortable to share the hurt they've caused in a particular situation, allow them to briefly share.)
> » Why is making amends just as important for you as for the people you've hurt?
> » What is it so difficult to say "I'm sorry?"

The leader of the group should close this time with a prayer that offers God thanks for the forgiveness he's already offered to us in our lives.

 **CLOSING**

Have your teenagers gather in a circle with their 3X5 cards. Ask them to close their eyes and hold their card. Then invite them to pray for God's help in following through on their commitment to make amends. When all who want to pray have done it, close in prayer, thanking

God for the freedom he brings through repentance. Encourage your students to keep their 3X5 card in a safe place.

Close by reading the Serenity Prayer together (available on p. 3 of their Student Journal). Keep in mind, some teenagers may not want to read aloud with the rest of the group. That's OK; encourage them to focus on the words being shared.

**God, grant me the serenity
to accept the things I cannot change,
the courage to change the things I can,
and the wisdom to know the difference.
Living one day at a time,
enjoying one moment at a time;
Accepting hardship as a pathway to peace;
Taking, as Jesus did,
this sinful world as it is;
Not as I would have it;
Trusting that you will make all things right
If I surrender to your will; So that I
may be reasonably happy in this life
and supremely happy with you forever
in the next. AMEN.**

- Reinhold Niebuhr

Don't forget to remind your students to spend time with their journals this week, reflecting on what God is teaching them during this journey.

Serve refreshments of some kind so kids and leaders can hang out and connect. Consider having some healthy options for those who may use food as a way of coping. A ping-pong table, foosball table, or even a few board games will give teenagers an excuse to connect.

AMENDS

lesson thirty-three

PRINCIPLE 6:

Evaluate all my relationships. Offer forgiveness to those who have hurt me and make amends for harm I've done to others, except when to do so would harm them or others.

SCRIPTURAL TRUTHS:

"Happy are the merciful" (Matthew 5:7 GNT).

"Happy are the peacemakers" (Matthew 5:9 GNT).

"Do to others as you would have them do to you" (Luke 6:31 NIV).

SCHEDULE

- **∴ CONNECT TIME** (15 minutes)
- **♫ WORSHIP** (10 minutes)
- **▌ TEACHING TIME** (35 minutes)
- **⚏ SMALL GROUPS** (40 minutes)
- **◑ CLOSING** (5 minutes)
- **∴ CONNECT TIME** (15 minutes)

SUPPLIES NEEDED

- » CD player (optional)
- » CD with worship music (optional)
- » 3X5 cards—one per teenager
- » Pens or pencils
- » A basket full of small, dirty rocks—small enough to fit in the palm of your hand, but big enough they can be written on
- » CD with soft background music (optional)
- » Pencils or chalk
- » Buckets of soapy water
- » Rags or sponges

PREPARATION

- » Pray for your teenagers and your meeting
- » Review this lesson
- » Gather supplies
- » Select songs for the Worship Time

••• CONNECT TIME

SUPPLIES: 3X5 cards, and pens or pencils.

Warmly welcome everyone to the group.

This is an opening "connect" activity that you're doing once every month. Have teenagers get in a circle. Give them each a 3X5 card and something to write with (if they don't already have a pen or pencil). Ask them to write one creative question on their card that's designed to discover what their friends in the group think, feel, and believe. For example: "If you lost your sense of smell, yet could still smell three things, what would they be?" Or "If you could only watch one TV show for the rest of your life, what would it be?"

Ask teenagers to pass the cards to you, then quickly select five question-cards based on which ones you think would be most interesting to answer. Then ask a teenager to volunteer to sit in a chair in the middle of your circle—the "Hot Seat." One by one, ask the Hot Seat person the five questions.

Encourage the remaining kids in the circle to ask at least two follow-up questions (total) after every answer from the Hot Seat person.

 # ♫ WORSHIP

Form pairs and ask them to discuss these questions.

ASK:
  » When was the last time you felt encouraged by someone?
  » What's the most powerful way to encourage people?

After a few minutes, gather together and **ASK:**
  » How has God encouraged you through your journey here at The Landing?

After a few teenagers answer, help them respond to God by leading three familiar worship songs. If you have a youth band, invite the group to lead your teenagers in worship. Otherwise, play the songs from a CD and encourage kids to sing along—or simply play the music as everyone sits and thinks about the words of the songs.

Then have everyone read aloud, together, this week's beatitudes: *"Happy are the merciful"* (Matthew 5:7 GNT) and *"Happy are the peacemakers"* (Matthew 5:9 GNT).

 # TEACHING TIME

SUPPLIES: a basket full of small rocks, pencils (or chalk, if it's easy to find), a few buckets of soapy water, some rags or sponges, and a CD with soft background music (optional). We encourage you to do this activity outside, or cover your floor with newspapers or towels.

This lesson is a little different from others—it's focused more on your teenagers acting on God's imperative to make amends for the hurts they've caused than on simply learning about it.

Gather in a circle and put the basket of rocks in the middle.

SAY: As we've mentioned before, we're on this journey on the road to healthier, freer lives. The reason we call this gathering The Landing is that this journey is like coming home to a place where you are loved and where you can be who God created you to be. This journey is for everyone who feels stuck in life—trapped by their hurts, hang-ups, and habits, or their circumstances, or their addictions. It's also a place for people who haven't faced those intense battles but want greater wisdom on leading a healthy life filled with freedom. The principles that we talk about are based on the beatitudes, where Jesus laid out principles for happiness in the sermon on the mount.

Sometimes the sins we carry around feel heavy, like rocks in our pockets. I'd like you to come forward and grab a few rocks, then go back to your seat and be quiet as you ask God to show you anything you've done or said in the last month that has been hurtful to others. As you think of things, use your pencil (or chalk) to write on one of the rocks a word that describes the hurt you've caused or the person you've hurt.

After five minutes or so, ask your teenagers to put their rocks in their pockets—or just hold the rocks if they don't have pockets.

Then SAY: Please join me in prayer. Father God, we're tired and weary from carrying these rocks around—the things we've done that have hurt others. We know you've said you'll carry our burdens, but sometimes we don't act as though we really believe you. Sometimes we're so afraid of what may happen if we admit what we've done and make amends for them, that we allow these things to hold us down. We're ready, God. We're willing to make amends for the harm we've caused others—to give our cares to you and trust that you'll know what to do with them. In Jesus' name, amen.

Bring out buckets of soapy water and rags or sponges and place them in the middle of the circle. Play some soft background music if you'd like to. Tell your teenagers to take their rocks from their pockets and clean them—not just the word they wrote, but also the dirt and grime from all corners and crevices. Give your kids plenty of time to do this to help them internalize the metaphor. As they work on their rocks, **SAY: What we're doing is a metaphor. It's not just about wiping dirt and pencil markings (or chalk) off a rock. It's about cleaning the dirt out of our own lives so that we can move on to making amends to the people we've hurt in our lives—so we can find the freedom to give to the people in our lives.**

As your young people finish cleaning their rocks, have them bring them forward to the middle of the circle and pile them. It's important that all rocks are cleaned. After all rocks have been cleaned and piled, read aloud 1 Peter 2:6: **"For in Scripture it says: 'See, I lay a stone in Zion, a chosen and precious cornerstone, and the one who trusts in him will never be put to shame.'"**

Then quickly read aloud **Ephesians 2:20: "...built on the foundation of the apostles and prophets, with Christ Jesus himself as the chief cornerstone."**

SMALL GROUPS

Prior to beginning your small group, read through the following Small Group Guidelines with your teenagers.

1. Focus on your own thoughts and feelings when sharing with the group.
2. Please avoid ALL cross talk.
3. We are here to support one another.
4. Value and protect anonymity and confidentiality.
5. Avoid offensive language; it has no place in a Christ-centered group.

Remember, as a leader you are to model these guidelines for your group as you lead the discussion.

Break your larger group into small groups of three or more, with a conversation leader in each one. To prime the pump for discussion, have the leaders begin the small group time by telling about a time (using their discretion) when they made amends with someone who caused them harm. Then have groups each discuss these questions (available on the CD-ROM).

Remember, as the leader, you may want to model some of these answers for your group by sharing from your own experience.

ASK:

» What are the components of making amends—in other words, what goes into it?

» It's sometimes obvious what we need to do to make amends to the person we've hurt. What do you do if it's not obvious?

» Has God revealed anyone that you need to make amends to that you didn't include on your Personal Inventory?

SAY: We've talked a lot about making amends—now it's time to act on it!

 **CLOSING**

Have your teenagers hold their rock in their hand.

SAY: Close your eyes and feel the weight of your rock in your hand. (Pause) Run your fingers over the rock, exploring its shape and its uniqueness. (Pause) You are unforgettable to God—he knows every one of your quirks and loves you for your uniqueness. (Pause) Now clench your hand around your rock. (Pause) God loves you with an unending love—he holds you in the strength of his palm. (Pause) Now spend a moment in silence, telling him whatever's on your heart.

Close by reading the Serenity Prayer together (available on p. 3 of their Student Journal). Keep in mind, some teenagers may not want to read aloud with the rest of the group. That's OK; encourage them to focus on the words being shared.

God, grant me the serenity
to accept the things I cannot change,
the courage to change the things I can,
and the wisdom to know the difference.
Living one day at a time,
enjoying one moment at a time;
Accepting hardship as a pathway to peace;
Taking, as Jesus did,
this sinful world as it is;
Not as I would have it;
Trusting that you will make all things right
If I surrender to your will; So that I
may be reasonably happy in this life
and supremely happy with you forever
in the next. AMEN.

- Reinhold Niebuhr

Don't forget to remind your students to spend time with their journals this week, reflecting on what God is teaching them during this journey.

⠿ CONNECT TIME

Serve refreshments of some kind so kids and leaders can hang out and connect. Consider having some healthy options for those who may use food as a way of coping. A ping-pong table, foosball table, or even a few board games will give teenagers an excuse to connect.

FORGIVENESS

lesson thirty-four

PRINCIPLE 6:

Evaluate all my relationships. Offer forgiveness to those who have hurt me and make amends for harm I've done to others, except when to do so would harm them or others.

SCRIPTURAL TRUTHS:

"Happy are the merciful" (Matthew 5:7 GNT).

"Happy are the peacemakers" (Matthew 5:9 GNT).

"Do to others as you would have them do to you"
(Luke 6:31 NIV).

"Therefore, if you are offering your gift at the altar and there remember that your brother has something against you, leave your gift there in front of the altar. First go and be reconciled to your brother; then come and offer your gift" (Matthew 5:23-24 NIV).

SCHEDULE

- **CONNECT TIME** (15 minutes)
- ♫ **WORSHIP** (15 minutes)
- **TEACHING TIME** (40 minutes)
- **SMALL GROUPS** (30 minutes)
- **CLOSING** (5 minutes)
- **CONNECT TIME** (15 minutes)

SUPPLIES NEEDED

- » CD player (optional)
- » CD with worship music (optional)
- » Bibles
- » 2 gallons of milk or water

PREPARATION

- » Pray for your teenagers and your meeting
- » Review this lesson
- » Gather supplies
- » Select songs for the Worship Time

CONNECT TIME

Warmly welcome everyone to the group.

Divide your teenagers into groups of three. Then have your kids introduce themselves to the other group members by saying their middle name and how/why they have that name. Then have each describe a favorite hobby they enjoyed when they were younger.

♫ WORSHIP

SAY: Tonight, we are going to look at forgiveness. As we begin to our time of worship, think about that word. Has there been a time when you've needed to ask someone—maybe God—for forgiveness? Has anyone ever had to ask you for your forgiveness?

Take a second to think about that time, and then we'll begin our time of worship.

Lead kids in three familiar worship songs. If you have a youth band, invite the group to lead your teenagers in worship. Otherwise, play the songs from a CD and encourage kids to sing along—or simply play the music as everyone sits and thinks about the words of the songs.

Then have everyone read aloud, together, this week's beatitude: *"Happy are the merciful" (Matthew 5:7 GNT) and "Happy are the peacemakers" (Matthew 5:9 GNT).*

 # ■ TEACHING TIME

SUPPLIES: 2 gallons of milk or water.

Have students form a circle; if you have a large group, they can remain in rows or at their tables. Ask for a volunteer to come forward. Give this person one of the gallons of milk or water, and have this teenager hold the container with both hands—permit the volunteer to hold whichever part of the container is most comfortable.

ASK:

» How long do you think you could hold that container in that position?

Then, hand the other container to the teenager. Have your volunteer hold one container in each hard—out to the sides, with arms extended, so this person looks like a "T."

ASK:

> » How about now? How long do you think you could stay like that?

Allow the volunteer to end whenever he or she has become too tired. Ask for more volunteers. Do this for 10-15 minutes—give as many students as possible a chance to participate. It won't be easy for most!

SAY: That wasn't easy, was it? I don't think many of us could have lasted very long like that. Imagine having to live your life like that. Imagine if this week I asked you to carry around those two gallons everywhere you went. It would be exhausting, wouldn't it?

The thing is, you and I carry heavy stuff around with us all of the time. The Bible calls these things burdens. Maybe your burdens are your worries. Maybe you're carrying around the knowledge that you've messed up in some pretty big ways. Maybe you're lugging around a grudge against someone who has hurt you. Whatever your burden is, wouldn't it feel so much better to get rid of it? A couple of weeks ago we began the process of letting go of things that were holding us back from becoming the people God has planned for us to be. Today we're going to look at how we can begin to let go of our burdens.

Have someone read Matthew 11:28-30.

ASK:
» What does this verse tell us about Jesus' ability to help us carry our burdens?

» Why do you think Jesus tells us he is gentle and humble?

SAY: Again, some of our burdens may be the wrong things we have done or the wrong things that have been done to us. When we talk about forgiveness, we're really talking about two things. We're talking about our need for forgiveness, and we're talking about our need to forgive other people. It's likely that you've been hurt in your life—maybe really badly. Maybe you've been abused or neglected or made to feel inferior. Because of this hurt, you may have decided to hold a grudge against the person who has hurt you. Remember the milk (or water) containers? How uncomfortable was it to hold on to those things? If you and I are going to get better, if we're going to be able to find freedom from our hurts, hang-ups, and habits, we are going to have to forgive those that have hurt us.

But why? One big reason is that you and I have needed and will need forgiveness.

Have someone read Romans 5:8.

SAY: That verse tells us that Jesus died for us before we got our acts together. Jesus died to forgive us. Let me change that, Jesus died to forgive me. Jesus died to forgive you.

And he did this over 2,000 years ago, long before any of us were even born. He paid the price to forgive our sins.

ASK:
> » If you have given your life to Jesus do you feel that forgiveness?
> » Why is it hard to accept that forgiveness?

SAY: So, if Jesus has forgiven us for the times we've blown it, we need to be willing to forgive other people when they've messed up, too. I'm not saying this will be easy, but it is necessary. Colossians 3:13 says, "Be gentle and ready to forgive; never hold grudges. Remember, the Lord forgave you, so you must forgive others."

The power to forgive those that have hurt us comes from Jesus and his forgiveness. Right now you may not feel like forgiving those that have hurt you. But you can begin the process of letting go of the grudge. Let's spend a couple of minutes praying silently, asking God to give us the ability to forgive.

SMALL GROUPS

Prior to beginning your small group, read through the following Small Group Guidelines with your teenagers.

1. Focus on your own thoughts and feelings when sharing with the group.
2. Please avoid ALL cross talk.
3. We are here to support one another.
4. Value and protect anonymity and confidentiality.
5. Avoid offensive language; it has no place in a Christ-centered group.

Remember, as a leader you are to model these guidelines for your group as you lead the discussion.

Break your larger group into small groups of three or more, with a conversation leader in each one. To prime the pump for discussion, have the leaders begin the small group time by telling about a time (using their discretion) when they forgave someone, or received forgiveness from someone. Then have groups each discuss these questions (available on the CD-ROM).

Remember, as the leader, you may want to model some of these answers for your group by sharing from your own experience.

ASK:

> » Is it sometimes hard to feel God's forgiveness when we've blown it? Why or why not?

» What's hard about offering forgiveness when you've been hurt? What's freeing about it?
» What's hard about receiving forgiveness when you've hurt someone? What's freeing about it?
» Have you forgiven yourself for the mistakes and bad choices from your past?
» Is forgiveness dependent on the person who's done the wrong being willing to say they are sorry first? Why or why not?

The leader of the group should close this time with a prayer that offers God thanks for the forgiveness he's already offered to us in our lives.

 **CLOSING**

Don't forget to remind your students to spend time with their journals this week, reflecting on what God is teaching them during this journey.

Close by reading the Serenity Prayer together (available on p. 3 of their Student Journal). Keep in mind, some teenagers may not want to read aloud with the rest of the group. That's OK; encourage them to focus on the words being shared.

> God, grant me the serenity
> to accept the things I cannot change,
> the courage to change the things I can,
> and the wisdom to know the difference.

Living one day at a time,
enjoying one moment at a time;
Accepting hardship as a pathway to peace;
Taking, as Jesus did,
this sinful world as it is;
Not as I would have it;
Trusting that you will make all things right
If I surrender to your will; So that I
may be reasonably happy in this life
and supremely happy with you forever
in the next. AMEN.

- Reinhold Niebuhr

::: CONNECT TIME

Serve refreshments of some kind so kids and leaders
can hang out and connect. Consider having some
healthy options for those who may use food as a way of
coping. A ping-pong table, foosball table, or even a few
board games will give teenagers an excuse to connect.

FORGIVENESS

lesson thirty-five

PRINCIPLE 6:

Evaluate all my relationships. Offer forgiveness to those who have hurt me and make amends for harm I've done to others, except when to do so would harm them or others.

SCRIPTURAL TRUTHS:

"Happy are the merciful" (Matthew 5:7 GNT).

"Happy are the peacemakers" (Matthew 5:9 GNT).

"Do to others as you would have them do to you" (Luke 6:31 NIV).

"Therefore, if you are offering your gift at the altar and there remember that your brother has something against you, leave your gift there in front of the altar. First go and be reconciled to your brother; then come and offer your gift" (Matthew 5:23-24 NIV).

SCHEDULE

- **CONNECT TIME** (15 minutes)
- ♫ **WORSHIP** (10 minutes)
- **TEACHING TIME** (35 minutes)
- **VIDEO TIME** (10 minutes)
- **SMALL GROUPS** (30 minutes)
- **CLOSING** (5 minutes)
- **CONNECT TIME** (15 minutes)

SUPPLIES NEEDED

» CD player (optional)
» CD with worship music (optional)
» TV and DVD player
» The Landing DVD 3
» 3X5 cards—plenty for each teenager
» Pens or pencils

PREPARATION

» Pray for your teenagers and your meeting
» Review this lesson
» Gather supplies
» Select songs for the Worship Time

 **CONNECT TIME**

Warmly welcome everyone to the group.

Have your teenagers and adult leaders stand in a circle and, one by one, quickly respond to a bizarre question. Each person gets just two seconds to think before responding—the whole group should count in unison "One thousand one, one thousand two" to count off the two seconds each person is allowed. If someone cannot answer within the two-second allowance, they're out of the circle. Create your own wacky questions, or use these as a starter.

ASK:

> » What's your favorite product that contains milk?
> » If you were a building, what would you be?
> » What's your favorite underarm deodorant, and which pit do you hit first?
> » What's your favorite chore around the house?
> » What's the grossest food you've ever eaten?

If you want, ask your teenagers to suggest their own wacky questions ahead of time.

♫ WORSHIP

Read aloud John 21:15-17, then **SAY: This interchange between Jesus and Peter happened after Jesus' resurrection from the dead, on a beach where Jesus cooked breakfast for Peter and the other disciples who'd been out fishing.**

ASK:

> » Why would Jesus ask Peter three times whether or not he loved him?

SAY: Maybe Jesus was giving Peter a chance to affirm his love three times, because Peter had denied Jesus three times before Jesus was crucified. It would be just like Jesus to want to "complete the circle of forgiveness" for Peter. Jesus is kind and good and wise—and he's on our side. Let's respond by telling him now how much we love him.

Then lead kids in three familiar worship songs. If you have a youth band, invite the group to lead your teenagers in worship. Otherwise, play the songs from a CD and encourage kids to sing along—or simply play the music as everyone sits and thinks about the words of the songs.

Then have everyone read aloud, together, this week's beatitudes: *"Happy are the merciful"* (Matthew 5:7 GNT) and *"Happy are the peacemakers"* (Matthew 5:9 GNT).

 **TEACHING TIME**

SUPPLIES: 3X5 cards, pens or pencils.

SAY: Last week we began looking at forgiveness. We talked about how all of us have people in our lives that we have hurt and that have hurt us. We saw that our power to forgive those that have hurt us comes from the forgiveness we have received from Jesus. Today we are going to work on releasing those who have hurt us and work toward forgiveness.

The thing is, it isn't always safe or even possible to offer our forgiveness face to face. For example, if you've been abused by someone, in order for you to find relief from that situation, you will need to forgive that person. But that doesn't mean that you need to open yourself up to be hurt again.

Or it could just be that the person that has harmed you has moved or that your offering of forgiveness could now create harm. Whatever the reason, offering forgiveness can be more an attitude of the heart than a face-to-face conversation.

Have the students each grab a stack of 3X5 cards and a pen or pencil. You may want to have extra cards stacked around the room so students can grab more if necessary. Have students each find a quiet place to have some room to themselves. Also, have them take out their inventories.

SAY: For the next few minutes we're going to spend some time getting ready to forgive those people that have hurt us. The truth is, offering forgiveness isn't always a one-time event. Sometimes we need to offer forgiveness several times to the people that have hurt us. Today may be the first time, or at least the first step.

Go ahead and look at your inventory sheets. If you don't have an inventory sheet, or this is your first time, think about someone who has harmed you in the past. It could be a friend, parent, family member, or someone else. We're going to spend some time being quiet. Begin this time by praying, asking God to help you begin to forgive the people from Column 1 of your inventory sheet. Next, look over those names and write a name down on one side of the card. Turn that card over and simply write, "I forgive you." Try to really mean it, too. If you don't feel like you're able to even write that down yet, write, "I want to forgive you." Sometimes the first step is to want to forgive.

Allow the students to take some time to do this; don't rush it. If someone finishes quickly, encourage that person to come up with a plan to offer the forgiveness face to face, if possible.

SAY: Make sure you put keep your cards in a safe place, but in a place where you can see them for the next few days. Flip through the cards and ask Jesus for the help to forgive the people whose names are on them. Every time you read one of the names say to yourself, "I forgive you."

📹 VIDEO TIME

Set up a DVD player and TV in your meeting area. Ahead of time, cue up the video "Joseph" from DVD 3 in the kit. Play the video—this one is 8:41 minutes long.

 SMALL GROUPS

After the whole group has watched the video, split into your small groups, with a conversation leader in each one. Have your conversation leaders ask these questions (available on the CD-ROM) about the video, with the intent to draw out personal stories from the kids in the group.

Remember, as the leader, you may want to model some of these answers for your group by sharing from your own experience.

ASK:

» As you watched the video, what impacted you the most? Explain.

» If you had been in Joseph's place, how do you think you would've reacted to your brothers?

» Why didn't Joseph immediately reveal who he was to his brothers?

» Describe a time when you forgave someone— what led up to that decision, and what happened after you forgave?

» Why can it be hard to forgive those who have hurt us?

At the end of this discussion, the leader should close in prayer, thanking God for cleansing us from our sins.

 **CLOSING**

Don't forget to remind your students to spend time with their journals this week, reflecting on what God is teaching them during this journey.

Close by reading the Serenity Prayer together (available on p. 3 of their Student Journal). Keep in mind, some teenagers may not want to read aloud with the rest of the group. That's OK; encourage them to focus on the words being shared.

God, grant me the serenity
to accept the things I cannot change,
the courage to change the things I can,
and the wisdom to know the difference.
Living one day at a time,
enjoying one moment at a time;

Accepting hardship as a pathway to peace;
Taking, as Jesus did,
this sinful world as it is;
Not as I would have it;
Trusting that you will make all things right
If I surrender to your will; So that I
may be reasonably happy in this life
and supremely happy with you forever
in the next. AMEN.

- Reinhold Niebuhr

 CONNECT TIME

Serve refreshments of some kind so kids and leaders can hang out and connect. Consider having some healthy options for those who may use food as a way of coping. A ping-pong table, foosball table, or even a few board games will give teenagers an excuse to connect.

CELEBRATION

lesson thirty-six

CELEBRATION

It's important to stop and celebrate with your teenagers! Use this week to do something fun with your group. Not only will your teenagers feel a sense of accomplishment, it's also a great opportunity to create community and friendships amongst your group.

Here are a few suggestions of ways to celebrate:

» **Movie Night:** Bring some snacks, pizza, soda, water, and other supplies and enjoy an appropriate movie together. To stay on the safe side, bring a rated G or PG movie to show your group. You know your students and your church better than we do, so make sure whatever you bring is appropriate for your setting.

» **Sporting Event:** This will require some planning ahead of time. If you have an amateur, college, or professional sports team nearby, plan on taking your group to one of their games.

» **Game Night:** Encourage teenagers to bring their favorite games with them. Again, make sure that the games they choose to bring are appropriate for your setting.

» **Family Fun Park:** If you have a local family fun park with miniature golf, bowling, or laser tag nearby, consider taking your kids there to celebrate. Playing together is just another way to continue to build trust and relationships.

Of course, you're not limited to these options. You know your teenagers better than we do, so do something that will be fun and memorable for them.

GRACE

lesson thirty-seven

PRINCIPLE 6:

Evaluate all my relationships. Offer forgiveness to those who have hurt me and make amends for harm I've done to others, except when to do so would harm them or others.

SCRIPTURAL TRUTHS:

"Happy are the merciful" (Matthew 5:7 GNT).

"Happy are the peacemakers" (Matthew 5:9 GNT).

"Therefore, if you are offering your gift at the altar and there remember that your brother has something against you, leave your gift there in front of the altar. First go and be reconciled to your brother; then come and offer your gift" (Matthew 5:23-24 NIV).

SCHEDULE

- ∴ **CONNECT TIME** (15 minutes)
- ♫ **WORSHIP** (15 minutes)
- 📖 **TEACHING TIME** (40 minutes)
- 👥 **SMALL GROUPS** (30 minutes)
- ⏰ **CLOSING** (5 minutes)
- ∴ **CONNECT TIME** (15 minutes)

SUPPLIES NEEDED

» CD player (optional)
» CD with worship music (optional)
» 3X5 cards — one per teenager
» Pens or pencils
» Sheets of newsprint, butcher paper, or poster board — one per three teenagers
» Markers
» Copies of the "Amazing Grace" lyrics (available on the CD-ROM)

PREPARATION

» Pray for your teenagers and your meeting
» Review this lesson
» Gather supplies
» Select songs for the Worship Time
» Make copies of the handout with "Amazing Grace" lyrics — one per student (available on the CD-ROM)

●●● CONNECT TIME

SUPPLIES: 3X5 cards, and pens or pencils.

Warmly welcome everyone to the group.

This is an opening "connect" activity that you're doing once every month. Have teenagers get in a circle. Give them each a 3X5 card and something to write with (if they don't already have a pen or pencil). Ask them to write one creative question on their card that's designed to discover what their friends in the group think, feel, and believe. For example: "Where is your most favorite place you've been?" Or "Do you have any phobias?"

Ask teenagers to pass the cards to you, then quickly select five question-cards based on which ones you think would be most interesting to answer. Then ask a teenager to volunteer to sit in a chair in the middle of your circle—the "Hot Seat." One by one, ask the Hot Seat person the five questions.

Encourage the remaining kids in the circle to ask at least two follow-up questions (total) after every answer from the Hot Seat person.

♫ WORSHIP

SUPPLIES: copies of the "Amazing Grace" lyrics handout.

Give each teenager a copy of the lyrics to "Amazing Grace" by John Newton. There are six verses, so count off by sixes until everyone in your group has a number. Tell them their number now corresponds to that number verse in the song—for example, if a teenager is a "three" then his assigned verse in the song is number three. Then have your kids rewrite their assigned verse in their own words, giving them a few minutes to do so.

Then have a volunteer who was assigned verse one stand and read the rewritten verse aloud. Go around the circle from one to six until the last person has shared. If you have a large group, you could ask for a few teenagers to share what they wrote.

Then lead kids in one or two familiar worship songs. If you have a youth band, invite the group to lead your teenagers in worship. Otherwise, play the songs from a CD and encourage kids to sing along—or simply play the music as everyone sits and thinks about the words of the songs.

Then have everyone read aloud, together, this week's beatitudes: *"Happy are the merciful" (Matthew 5:7 GNT)* and *"Happy are the peacemakers" (Matthew 5:9 GNT).*

 **TEACHING TIME**

SUPPLIES: sheets of newsprint, butcher paper, or poster board; and markers.

ASK:
> » In the last two weeks, who has received a grade for a test or school project?
> » Did you feel better or worse about yourself because of that grade? Why?

After you've heard from a few of your teenagers, **SAY:** The big question lurking behind the grades we get is often, "Do I measure up?" Grades have a lot of power over us, typically—it's easy to believe that the grades we get for *what we do* are actually grades for *who we are*, right?

Form trios, and give each group a marker and a sheet of newsprint, butcher paper, or poster board. Then **SAY:** In your group, select a celebrity to grade—it could be a movie or TV star, a musician, a politician, or an athlete. You decide on the grading criteria, and then award that person the actual grade. Be prepared to defend your grade and the criteria you used to arrive at it. Use the newsprint and markers to make a giant-size report card to present.

As groups work, walk around and **ASK** questions such as:
  » Why did you choose that as a grading criterion?
  » How can you be sure you're grading fairly?
  » How do teachers ensure fairness in grading?

After 10 minutes or so, ask groups to each choose a spokesperson. Then **SAY:** Each spokesperson will present his or her group's celebrity grade and criteria. After the presentation, others who disagree with the grade can challenge it. Any member of the presenting group can respond to the challenges.

After each group has presented and then defended its celebrity grade and criteria, **ASK:**
  » What positive value do grades have?
  » What negative impact can they have?
  » How much do grades really determine a person's worth?

» How much do your answers reflect reality?

Then have trios explore what God has to say about grading. Give each trio one of the following Scripture references to look up and discuss, then develop a report card criterion based on it—in other words, how might this verse or passage be used to evaluate or grade us in life? The groups should use the other side of the newsprint, butcher paper, or poster board for this:
» 1 Corinthians 3:8
» 1 Corinthians 15:58
» Ephesians 6:5-8
» Philippians 1:21-22
» 2 Timothy 2:15

If you have more than five groups of three, simply duplicate assigned passages.

Have trios each write their Scripture reference on top of their newsprint, butcher paper, or poster board, followed by the grading criteria extracted from the reference. Then have a spokesperson from each group read its Scripture reference and present the group's grading criteria.

Then **ASK:**
» How do these "grading criteria" compare to the typical ways you're graded in life?
» If teachers graded your schoolwork the same way God grades our lives, how would you do? Explain.
» What's your definition of "grace"?

» How is that definition similar to and different from your definition of "grading"?

Then **SAY:** Let me share a few facts you've maybe never heard. Albert Einstein didn't speak until he was 3 years old. Thomas Edison was excused from school because he was deemed unteachable. Walt Disney got fired from one of his early jobs for "having no good ideas." If they had listened to their "grades," we might never have known the theory of relativity, or enjoyed electric lighting, or enjoyed any of those classic Disney movies. The only person who can grade us fairly is the One who made us—and God uses grace as his "grading criteria." The key Scripture truth we look to here at The Landing is 2 Corinthians 12:9-10: "But he said to me, 'My grace is enough for you. When you are weak, my power is made perfect in you.' So I am very happy to brag about my weaknesses. Then Christ's power can live in me. For this reason I am happy when I have weaknesses, insults, hard times, sufferings, and all kinds of troubles for Christ. Because when I am weak, then I am truly strong."

ASK:
» Why does our weakness make us strong?
» Grace means that we're consciously dependent upon God instead of ourselves. What's one way you've learned to depend on God instead of yourself?

Close by reading Romans 8:35-39 with your group.

SMALL GROUPS

Prior to beginning your small group, read through the following Small Group Guidelines with your teenagers.

1. Focus on your own thoughts and feelings when sharing with the group.
2. Please avoid ALL cross talk.
3. We are here to support one another.
4. Value and protect anonymity and confidentiality.
5. Avoid offensive language; it has no place in a Christ-centered group.

Remember, as a leader you are to model these guidelines for your group as you lead the discussion.

Break your larger group into small groups of three or more, with a conversation leader in each one. To prime the pump for discussion, have the leaders begin the small group time by telling about a time (using their discretion) when they gave or received grace. Then have groups each discuss these questions (available on the CD-ROM).

Remember, as the leader, you may want to model some of these answers for your group by sharing from your own experience.

ASK:

» Why are "bad grades" so hard to accept?

» Whose "grade" means the most to you—parents, friends, teachers, or another specific group of people? Why?

» Why do so many of us seem to struggle with receiving grace?

» Why does it so often seem better to us to work our way out of our problems, rather than receive God's grace for them?

» Do you grade others the same way you grade yourself? Why or why not?

» How is God's "grading system" different from your own?

The leader of the group should close this time with a prayer that offers God thanks for his grace.

 **CLOSING**

Don't forget to remind your students to spend time with their journals this week, reflecting on what God is teaching them during this journey.

Close by reading the Serenity Prayer together (available on p. 3 of their Student Journal). Keep in mind, some teenagers may not want to read aloud with the rest of the group. That's OK; encourage them to focus on the words being shared.

God, grant me the serenity
to accept the things I cannot change,
the courage to change the things I can,
and the wisdom to know the difference.
Living one day at a time,
enjoying one moment at a time;
Accepting hardship as a pathway to peace;
Taking, as Jesus did,
this sinful world as it is;
Not as I would have it;
Trusting that you will make all things right
If I surrender to your will; So that I
may be reasonably happy in this life
and supremely happy with you forever
in the next. AMEN.

- Reinhold Niebuhr

 CONNECT TIME

Serve refreshments of some kind so kids and leaders
can hang out and connect. Consider having some
healthy options for those who may use food as a way of
coping. A ping-pong table, foosball table, or even a few
board games will give teenagers an excuse to connect.

GRACE

lesson thirty-eight

PRINCIPLE 6:

Evaluate all my relationships. Offer forgiveness to those who have hurt me and make amends for harm I've done to others, except when to do so would harm them or others.

SCRIPTURAL TRUTHS:

"Happy are the merciful" (Matthew 5:7 GNT).

"Happy are the peacemakers" (Matthew 5:9 GNT).

"Therefore, if you are offering your gift at the altar and there remember that your brother has something against you, leave your gift there in front of the altar. First go and be reconciled to your brother; then come and offer your gift" (Matthew 5:23-24 NIV).

SCHEDULE

- ⋮⋮ **CONNECT TIME** (15 minutes)
- 🎵 **WORSHIP** (10 minutes)
- 📖 **TEACHING TIME** (30 minutes)
- 🎥 **VIDEO TIME** (15 minutes)
- 👥 **SMALL GROUPS** (30 minutes)
- ⏰ **CLOSING** (5 minutes)
- ⋮⋮ **CONNECT TIME** (15 minutes)

SUPPLIES NEEDED

- » CD player (optional)
- » CD with worship music (optional)
- » TV and DVD player
- » The Landing DVD 3
- » Paper
- » Pens or pencils
- » Bibles
- » A few blindfolds—you can use old T-shirts, bandanas, or other material
- » Envelopes—one per teenager

PREPARATION

- » Pray for your teenagers and your meeting
- » Review this lesson
- » Gather supplies
- » Select songs for the Worship Time

∴ CONNECT TIME

SUPPLIES: paper, and pens or pencils.

Warmly welcome everyone to the group.

Form teams of three. Give each team a sheet of paper and a pen or pencil. Challenge teams to list things members don't have in common—things that make each person unique. For example, they may have been born in different states, might go to different schools, or might like different music.

Tell teams they have three minutes to create their lists, so they need to work quickly. Warn them when they have one minute left, and when they have 30 seconds left.

When time is up, find out which team has the longest list and ask team members to read the "uncommon" things they listed.

Then **ASK:**
   » How easy or hard was it to discover things that you and your team members don't have in common?
   » Do our uncommon things make it harder or easier to build community here at The Landing?
   » How can our uncommon things actually draw us closer together?

🎵 WORSHIP

Lead kids in three familiar worship songs. If you have a youth band, invite the group to lead your teenagers in worship. Otherwise, play the songs from a CD and encourage kids to sing along—or simply play the music as everyone sits and thinks about the words of the songs.

Then have everyone read aloud, together, this week's beatitude: *"Happy are the merciful" (Matthew 5:7 GNT) and "Happy are the peacemakers" (Matthew 5:9 GNT).*

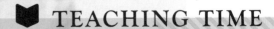

SUPPLIES: Bibles, a few blindfolds, paper, envelopes, and pens or pencils.

Pile the blindfolds just outside of your meeting room door.

Explain that in this lesson at The Landing you'll dive into the story of a blind man. Ask one teenager to leave the room, pick up a blindfold outside, and put it on while outside of the room—and then come back in blindfolded. When that person enters, the other kids who haven't been blindfolded yet should give instructions on how to return to his or her seat. (If you have a large group, have only a few kids do this activity for the sake of time.) Once that person is seated, have the next person go out of the room to be blindfolded.

After a number of kids have come in blindfolded and made their way to their seats, have them remove their blindfolds, then **ASK:**

> » Other than not being able to see, what was hard about this activity?

After your teenagers respond, **SAY:** Blindness is an obvious limitation. But each one of us has limitations—things that hamper us or challenge us.

ASK:
> » What are some less obvious limitations that people have to face in life?

After kids respond, **SAY:** As we listen to a story about a blind man, remember we all have things we wish we could change about ourselves. We all have limitations. We're all in need of God's grace.

Read aloud Mark 10:46-48, and then **ASK:**
> » Bartimaeus asks Jesus for mercy. What does "mercy" mean to you?

Then **ASK:**
> » Bartimaeus was determined to see Jesus. Why do many people decide to just live with their limitations instead of stopping at nothing to get whole or healed?

Read aloud Mark 10:49-51, then **ASK:**
> » It's obvious what Bartimaeus wants—so why does Jesus basically require him to state the obvious?

Read aloud Mark 10:51-52, then **ASK:**
> » Bartimaeus is free to go, but he decides to follow Jesus instead—why?

SAY: Notice that Jesus heals him and tells him to "go"—no strings attached. Sometimes we think we have to earn Jesus' favor to get his mercy, but instead he gives us undeserved kindness. We don't have to "pay him back" for what he's done for us—his grace is a free gift, and he wants our response to be something we offer freely.

Jesus isn't asking just Bartimaeus, "What do you want me to do for you?" He's asking us the same question.

Give each kid a piece of paper, an envelope, and a pen or pencil. Then ask everyone to write a letter to Jesus, answering the question he asked Bartimaeus: "What do you want me to do for you?" Have kids each put their letters in an envelope, seal it, and put their name on it. Reassure your teenagers that their letters will remain sealed, and that no one will read these letters. Collect the envelopes and hold on to them until the final meeting of The Landing—then give them back to your teenagers to open. At that time, you'll be inviting them to share any "answer" they've received.

SAY: Jesus wants to heal us, to give us the grace we need to experience a right relationship with him. He wants a relationship with us. However, his grace is a free gift—it isn't something we can earn. God loved you and me while we were still out there sinning. Romans 5:8 says, "God demonstrates his own love for us in this: While we were still sinners, Christ died for us." We can, in turn, love others because God first loved us. We can also forgive others because God first forgave us. Colossians 3:13

says, "Be gentle and ready to forgive; never hold grudges. Remember, the Lord forgave you, so you must forgive others."

VIDEO TIME

Set up a DVD player and TV in your meeting area. Ahead of time, cue up the video "Grace, We Just Don't Get It" from DVD 3 in the kit. Play the video—this one is 15:25 long.

SMALL GROUPS

Prior to beginning your small group, read through the following Small Group Guidelines with your teenagers.

1. Focus on your own thoughts and feelings when sharing with the group.
2. Please avoid ALL cross talk.
3. We are here to support one another.
4. Value and protect anonymity and confidentiality.
5. Avoid offensive language; it has no place in a Christ-centered group.

Remember, as a leader you are to model these guidelines for your group as you lead the discussion.

After the whole group has watched the video, split into your small groups, with a conversation leader in each one. Have your conversation leaders ask these questions (available on the CD-ROM) about the video, with the intent to draw out personal stories from the kids in the group.

Remember, as the leader, you may want to model some of these answers for your group by sharing from your own experience.

ASK:

- » As you watched the video, what impacted you the most? Explain.
- » What's something about grace that you "just don't get"?
- » When have you experienced grace from someone—something that made a big difference in your life?
- » When have you offered grace to someone— something that changed that person's life?
- » When have you "tasted" God's grace—what happened, and how is it still impacting you today?

At the end of this discussion, the leader should close in prayer, thanking God for his grace.

 **CLOSING**

Don't forget to remind your students to spend time with their journals this week, reflecting on what God is teaching them during this journey.

Close by reading the Serenity Prayer together (available on p. 3 of their Student Journal). Keep in mind, some teenagers may not want to read aloud with the rest of the group. That's OK; encourage them to focus on the words being shared.

God, grant me the serenity
to accept the things I cannot change,
the courage to change the things I can,
and the wisdom to know the difference.
Living one day at a time,
enjoying one moment at a time;
Accepting hardship as a pathway to peace;
Taking, as Jesus did,
this sinful world as it is;
Not as I would have it;
Trusting that you will make all things right
If I surrender to your will; So that I
may be reasonably happy in this life
and supremely happy with you forever
in the next. AMEN.

- Reinhold Niebuhr

••• CONNECT TIME

Serve refreshments of some kind so kids and leaders can hang out and connect. Consider having some healthy options for those who may use food as a way of coping. A ping-pong table, foosball table, or even a few board games will give teenagers an excuse to connect.

PRAYER STATIONS

lesson thirty-nine

PRINCIPLE 6:

Evaluate all my relationships. Offer forgiveness to those who have hurt me and make amends for harm I've done to others, except when to do so would harm them or others.

SCRIPTURAL TRUTHS:

"Happy are the merciful" (Matthew 5:7 GNT).

"Happy are the peacemakers" (Matthew 5:9 GNT).

"Therefore, if you are offering your gift at the altar and there remember that your brother has something against you, leave your gift there in front of the altar. First go and be reconciled to your brother; then come and offer your gift" (Matthew 5:23-24 NIV).

SCHEDULE

🔖 **PRAYER STATIONS** (90 minutes)

⁙ **CONNECT TIME** (30 minutes)

SUPPLIES NEEDED

- » CD player (optional)
- » CD with soft background music (optional)
- » Station Instructions (one for each station)
- » Newsprint (or butcher paper)
- » Tape
- » Markers
- » Pens
- » Bread, cup, and juice for communion

PREPARATION

- » Pray for your teenagers and your meeting
- » Review this lesson
- » Gather supplies
- » Set up each station

 # PRAYER STATIONS

SUPPLIES: CD player, CD with soft background music; station instructions (one for each station); newsprint (or butcher paper); tape; markers; pens; and bread, cup, and juice for communion.

As you play soft background music, warmly welcome everyone to the group.

SAY: This is going to be different from our typical gathering here at The Landing. We'll be spending the majority of our night in thought and prayer, as well as evaluating where we are in our personal journeys through The Landing. If you look around the room, you'll see that we have set up three stations for you to work through. Each station has a printed instruction sheet nearby so make sure you read those instructions when you visit each station. Of course, if you have any questions, please ask!

I want to point out the importance of Station 3. At that station, we'll be offering communion. If you've been around the church for a while, you might have heard this word, or even participated in taking communion. Basically, communion is something that Christians do to remember the sacrifice that Jesus made for us on the cross.

At that station, you'll find a passage from the Bible that basically explains what communion is and how important it is. You'll also find bread, and some juice. The bread symbolizes Jesus' body. In 1 Corinthians 11, we are reminded that Jesus said, "This is my body, which is for you; do this in remembrance of me." The juice symbolizes Jesus' blood. He said, "This cup is the new covenant in my blood; do this, whenever you drink it, in remembrance of me."

This station is here for those of you that want to participate in communion. If you don't feel comfortable, or you just don't want to, that's fine! This isn't something that should be forced, but for those of you who decide to partake, please focus on the enormity of Jesus' words.

When you're done with all of the stations, feel free to hang out, chat with your friends, or if you want, write some thoughts down on your journal. However, please keep your voices down as others may still be working through the stations.

STATION 1
Printed Instructions (available on the CD-ROM)

Journal Station
Take your personal inventory and thank God for all of the people that you've already made amends to or offered forgiveness to.

STATION 2
Take a large piece of newsprint (or butcher paper) and tape it on a wall near your station. Write the words "I'm thankful for..." at the top.

Printed Instructions (available on the CD-ROM)

Gratitude List
Spend some time thinking through what you're grateful for. Some of these things may include your friends, family, God's mercy or grace, your teachers, some special possessions, or even your health. After you've thought through some of these things, grab a marker and write the reasons you're grateful on the paper taped to the board. Include as much or as little as you'd like.

STATION 3
Printed Instructions (available on the CD-ROM)

23For I received from the Lord what I also passed on to you: The Lord Jesus, on the night he was betrayed, took bread, 24and when he had given thanks, he broke it and said, "This is my body, which is for you; do this in remembrance of me." 25In the same way, after supper he took the cup, saying, "This cup is the new covenant in my blood; do this, whenever you drink it, in remembrance of me." 26For whenever you eat this bread and drink this cup, you proclaim the Lord's death until he comes.

27Therefore, whoever eats the bread or drinks the cup of the Lord in an unworthy manner will be guilty of sinning against the body and blood of the Lord. 28A man ought to examine himself before he eats of the bread and drinks of the cup (1 Corinthians 11:23-28).

Take some time to read and think through this passage and what Jesus is saying. When you're ready, feel free to take part of the bread, remembering Jesus' symbolic words as you put it in your mouth. Next, take some of the juice, remembering what it represents as you put it in your mouth.

Close your time, by silently reading the Serenity Prayer (available on pp. 3 of the Student Journal).

∴ CONNECT TIME

Serve refreshments of some kind so kids and leaders can hang out and connect. Consider having some healthy options for those who may use food as a way of coping. A ping-pong table, foosball table, or even a few board games will give teenagers an excuse to connect.

CROSSROADS

lesson forty

PRINCIPLE 7:

Reserve a daily time with God for self-examination, Bible reading, and prayer in order to know God and his will for my life and to gain the power to follow his will.

SCRIPTURAL TRUTHS:

"So, if you think you are standing firm, be careful that you don't fall!" (1 Corinthians 10:12 NIV).

SCHEDULE

- ⋰ **CONNECT TIME** (15 minutes)
- ♫ **WORSHIP** (15 minutes)
- 📖 **TEACHING TIME** (40 minutes)
- 👥 **SMALL GROUPS** (30 minutes)
- ⏰ **CLOSING** (5 minutes)
- ⋰ **CONNECT TIME** (15 minutes)

SUPPLIES NEEDED

» CD player (optional)
» CD with worship music (optional)
» Bibles
» 3X5 cards
» Pens

PREPARATION

» Pray for your teenagers and your meeting
» Review this lesson
» Gather supplies
» Select songs for the Worship Time

 **CONNECT TIME**

Warmly welcome everyone to the group.

Here's one you've done before. Have your teenagers and adult leaders stand in a circle and, one by one, quickly respond to a bizarre question. Each person gets just two seconds to think before responding—the whole group should count in unison "One thousand one, one thousand two" to count off the two seconds each person is allowed. If someone cannot answer within the two-second allowance, they're out of the circle. Create your own wacky questions, or use these as a starter:

» **What are your hidden talents?**
» **Who was your favorite singer or band when you were in elementary school?**
» **Have you broken any bones? If so, how many? How?**

» What is the best prank that you've pulled on someone?

» What is the best prank that someone has pulled on you?

If you want, ask your teenagers to suggest their own wacky questions ahead of time.

 # WORSHIP

Ask your teenagers to find a partner. Have them think about a big or small decision that they need to make. It could be anything. Then ask them to brainstorm for each other all the pros and cons for the choices they could make with that decision: "On the one hand," "but on the other hand." Have them continue until they've exhausted all the possible pros and cons.

SAY: One way to worship God is to include him in our conversations rather than simply thinking through tough decisions on our own. Take a minute to talk about how your partner helped you with your decision. Then take a minute to pray, either together or silently by yourself, and ask for the courage to make the choice to include God in all of your decisions.

Then, lead kids in two or three familiar worship songs. If you have a youth band, invite the group to lead your teenagers in worship. Otherwise, play the songs from a CD and encourage kids to sing along—or simply play the music as everyone sits and thinks about the words of the songs.

Then have everyone read aloud, together, this week's scriptural truth: *"So, if you think you are standing firm, be careful that you don't fall!" (1 Corinthians 10:12 NIV).*

 **TEACHING TIME**

SUPPLIES: 3X5 cards and pens.

SAY: We're going to play a game you might have played as little children. It's called "Red Light, Green Light." You remember that you're supposed to move forward when we yell out, "Green Light," and you're supposed to stop when we call out, "Red Light." Let's make it a little more challenging and ask you to hop on one foot. Use the foot that is the opposite one from your dominant hand. (For example, if you are right-handed, hop on your left foot.) Sometimes we'll tell you to change the position of your bodies, and sometimes we'll ask you to move to the right or to the left or to go backward, so you'll have to listen carefully to the directions. (Close your eyes. Green Light. Red Light. Hop on the opposite foot. Red Light. Green Light. Red Light. Get down on your hands and knees. And so on.)

Let one teenager take a turn yelling out the directions while you have rest of the teenagers line up across the back of the room. Let a couple of teenagers take turns leading the game while asking different ways to make the game challenging; eyes closed, getting on hands and knees, and so on.

SAY: As you can see, you had to continually decide to "stop" or "go" and you had to keep changing directions. As much as this game might have made you feel like little kids again, you could see that sometimes it wasn't very easy to quickly figure out where you were going or if you had to go at all! That's a lot like life. Sometimes it's hard for all of us to figure out if we're supposed to go forward, stay, or go backward.

In your journey here at the Landing, you've made a lot of changes. In Principle 1, you faced some of the hurts, hang-ups, and habits in your life and got real about what's wrong and what's right in your life. In Principle 2, you started to believe that God has the power to help you change, and in Principle 3, you gave your life to Jesus. Then came Principle 4, where you took a good, thorough look at your life—the good and the not so good—and came clean about it. In Principle 5, you let go of some of the things keeping you back from being the person God wants you to be. In Principle 6, you looked at your relationships, said sorry for the things you did to hurt other people, and forgave people who have hurt you.

Now you're at a crossroads in your journey. When
we reach this seventh principle, we're not done at
all! We still have some major decisions to make.
We have been examining ourselves for weeks. But
the self-examination continues! We have to start
deciding if we want to continue on our journey and
move forward, or if we're just too tired of doing the
work and want to rest and stay at the same place. Or
if this has all been too hard, maybe we're tempted to
go backward to what has been comfortable for us,
backward to our hurts, hang-ups, and habits.

Read Luke 9:1-17.

ASK:

» When the disciples did not know how to feed the
crowd, what did they do and why?

» How does this passage of Scripture relate to us?

» Have you made the decision to move forward
on the journey, to rest for a while, or to go
backward? If you're comfortable sharing with us,
why have you made that choice?

» How will asking Jesus to guide us on this journey
help us?

SAY: Now think about your current crossroad—the
big decision or decisions you're facing right now.
(Pass out the 3X5 cards) Write down on this card a
big decision you are struggling with. Draw an arrow
to the right to indicate if you like you've been going
forward, a line without any arrow to indicate that

you're staying the same, or an arrow to the left to indicate that you're moving backward. Take a few minutes to think about the pros and cons and to pray about this decision.

 ## SMALL GROUPS

Prior to beginning your small group, read through the following Small Group Guidelines with your teenagers.

1. Focus on your own thoughts and feelings when sharing with the group.
2. Please avoid ALL cross talk.
3. We are here to support one another.
4. Value and protect anonymity and confidentiality.
5. Avoid offensive language; it has no place in a Christ-centered group.

Remember, as a leader you are to model these guidelines for your group as you lead the discussion.

Break your larger group into small groups of three or more, with a conversation leader in each one. To prime the pump for discussion, have the leaders begin the small group time by telling about a time (using their discretion) when they faced a crossroads in their life. Then have groups each discuss these questions (available on the CD-ROM).

Remember, as the leader, you may want to model some of these answers for your group by sharing from your own experience.

ASK:

» What have you observed about the way most people make big decisions? What do you like and not like about that?

» Why do some people seem to change in life, while others seem stuck forever in their old patterns?

» Can you choose one time every day where you can connect with Jesus? What time of day works best for you and why?

» What's one way you feel like you're at a crossroad in your life right now? Explain.

» From your perspective, what are some of the strategies for sticking to the positive changes you want in your life?

 ## CLOSING

SAY: We're at a crossroads at the Landing right now. We've got some choices to make with the direction we're going to take from this point on. But we're not alone; we're all together in this as a team. We have each other to help us move forward.

Close by reading the Serenity Prayer together (available on p. 3 of their Student Journal). Keep in mind, some teenagers may not want to read aloud with the rest of the group. That's OK; encourage them to focus on the words being shared.

God, grant me the serenity
to accept the things I cannot change,
the courage to change the things I can,
and the wisdom to know the difference.
Living one day at a time,
enjoying one moment at a time;
Accepting hardship as a pathway to peace;
Taking, as Jesus did,
this sinful world as it is;
Not as I would have it;
Trusting that you will make all things right
If I surrender to your will; So that I
may be reasonably happy in this life
and supremely happy with you forever
in the next. AMEN.

- Reinhold Niebuhr

Don't forget to remind your students to spend time with their journals this week, reflecting on what God is teaching them during this journey.

⋮ CONNECT TIME

Serve refreshments of some kind so kids and leaders can hang out and connect. Consider having some healthy options for those who may use food as a way of coping. A ping-pong table, foosball table, or even a few board games will give teenagers an excuse to connect.

CROSSROADS

lesson forty-one

CROSSROADS lesson forty-one

PRINCIPLE 7:

Reserve a daily time with God for self-examination, Bible reading, and prayer in order to know God and his will for my life and to gain the power to follow his will.

SCRIPTURAL TRUTHS:

"So, if you think you are standing firm, be careful that you don't fall!" (1 Corinthians 10:12 NIV).

SCHEDULE

- **CONNECT TIME** (15 minutes)
- **WORSHIP** (10 minutes)
- **TEACHING TIME** (35 minutes)
- **VIDEO TIME** (12 minutes)
- **SMALL GROUPS** (30 minutes)
- **CLOSING** (3 minutes)
- **CONNECT TIME** (15 minutes)

SUPPLIES NEEDED

- » CD player (optional)
- » CD with worship music (optional)
- » TV and DVD player
- » The Landing DVD 3
- » Bibles
- » Paper
- » Markers

PREPARATION

- » Pray for your teenagers and your meeting
- » Review this lesson
- » Gather supplies
- » Select songs for the Worship Time

 **CONNECT TIME**

SUPPLIES: Paper and markers.

Warmly welcome everyone to the group.

Give each teenager a piece of paper and a marker. Have them draw the shape of a license plate on their paper.

SAY: You've all seen personalized license plates on cars. For example, "PowdrHd" shows that the car owner is an avid skier. Or 10SNE1—"Tennis, anyone?"—shows that the person is really into tennis. Take a few minutes right now to create your own custom-made license plate that tells something about who you are.

After about five minutes, go around the group and have kids guess what each license plate says or means; then have that person explain the meaning behind the plate.

♫ WORSHIP

Lead kids in three familiar worship songs. If you have a youth band, invite the group to lead your teenagers in worship. Otherwise, play the songs from a CD and encourage kids to sing along—or simply play the music as everyone sits and thinks about the words of the songs.

Then have everyone read aloud, together, this week's scriptural truth: *"So, if you think you are standing firm, be careful that you don't fall!" (1 Corinthians 10:12 NIV).*

■ TEACHING TIME

SUPPLIES: Bibles.

SAY: We're going to play a game tonight that you may not have played for a long time. It's called "Telephone." If you don't remember the game it works like this. We'll all get in a circle and I'll start by whispering something to the person on my left. He or she will then repeat what I said to the person to their left and so on until it gets back to me. Then we'll see how close we get. No one is allowed to repeat the sentence.

Try to make these hard; here are some suggested phrases:

> » I'll take a large pizza with pepperoni and onions.
> » You may think you know, but you don't know.
> » The last time I saw that guy, he wore a purple shirt with white jeans.

ASK:

> » How did we do?
> » How confident were you that the listener heard your statement clearly?
> » Is that an effective form of communication?

SAY: I think if you and I could only communicate that way, we'd never really get to know each other. Isn't it so much easier to hear directly from the person we're talking to? Think about your best friend. If you and your best friend never spent time talking—in person or on the phone—you'd never really know what they were like, what they were into. And when you did talk, if one of you spent all of the time talking without listening to the other person, would you ever really know what they were like?

Many of us complain that we never get to hear from God. We hear stories like Moses in the Old Testament where God spoke audibly and we think, "If I could hear from God like that, I'd do whatever he asked." And the truth is, most of us don't get to hear from God in that way.

ASK:

» Does this mean we never get to hear from God?

» If we agree that we can hear from God, how do you think he talks to us?

» Have you ever "heard" God? If you feel comfortable, explain.

SAY: Just like in our friendships, if we don't spend time talking to and listening to God, how can we expect to hear from him? There are a couple of ways that we can practice hearing from God: prayer and Bible reading.

Prayer is simply talking to God. Jesus spent all kinds of time talking to God, and he showed us how we can, too. In fact, Hebrews 4:16 says, "Let us then approach the throne of grace with confidence, so that we may receive mercy and find grace to help us in our time of need."

ASK:

» How is prayer like "approaching the throne of grace"?

» Do you ever feel weird about praying? Why or why not?

SAY: I'd like to give us all a chance to practice praying out loud. I know for some of you that feels strange. Some of you may not feel comfortable praying in front of other people. That's OK. We're all going to pray out loud at the same time. Instead of taking turns or going around the circle, we'll all pray together. Talk to God about whatever you want. We'll only do it for a minute or so, and I'll get your attention when it's time to stop.

I'll open us in prayer: Dear God, we are all here today because we want to know you better. You know our hearts. Some of us have a hard time praying to you. We don't always know what to say. But right now we're going to lift our voices to you in prayer.

Now you, go ahead and pray, out loud.

After a minute or so, close the prayer. You may need to speak up to get kids' attention over the sound of the prayers.

ASK:
» How did that feel?
» Was it hard to pray while others prayed?
» Do you think God could hear each of our voices?

SAY: Another other way to learn to hear God's voice is by reading his Word, the Bible. People have described the Bible as God's love letter to us, a road map, and a user's guide to life. Psalm 119:105 says, "Your word will be a guide to my feet and a light to my path." As we talked about last week, we're at this point where we can decide to move forward or we can stall and end up going backward into our old hurts, hang-ups, and habits. Reading the Bible daily will help us move forward, as we allow God's Word to guide our feet and light our path.

ASK:

» Have you ever read anything in the Bible and felt like God was speaking directly to you? Explain.
» If you've never read the Bible, are you unsure of where to start?

Hold up a Bible.

SAY: When we approach the Bible we can be intimidated. There are different books, chapters, and verses, not to mention two different Testaments. It can be confusing.

Many people never start reading the Bible because they don't know where to start. I'd suggest you get started in the New Testament, which is the account of the life of Jesus and his ministry and the work of his followers following his death and resurrection. The books of Matthew, Mark, Luke, and John are called Gospels, because they have the "good news" of Jesus and his life.

But the main thing is, just start, and then keep reading. If all of this is stuff you already know, just keep reading your Bibles. Make it a part of your everyday life. Set aside some time, everyday, for you and God. Spend time praying. Don't just do all of the talking, but give God some time to respond. That means listen. Stop and be quiet for a while. It might feel strange at first, it might be hard to fit it in to your schedule, but once you begin this healthy habit, you'll experience a closeness with God. That closeness will lead you to trust him more, and to know him more.

 VIDEO TIME

Set up a DVD player and TV in your meeting area. Ahead of time, cue up the video "What Keeps You From Following God?" from DVD 3 in the kit. Play the video—this one is 11:38 minutes long.

SMALL GROUPS

Prior to beginning your small group, read through the following Small Group Guidelines with your teenagers.

1. Focus on your own thoughts and feelings when sharing with the group.
2. Please avoid ALL cross talk.
3. We are here to support one another.
4. Value and protect anonymity and confidentiality.
5. Avoid offensive language; it has no place in a Christ-centered group.

Remember, as a leader you are to model these guidelines for your group as you lead the discussion.

After the whole group has watched the video, split into your small groups, with a conversation leader in each one. Have your conversation leaders ask these questions (available on the CD-ROM) about the video, with the intent to draw out personal stories from the kids in the group.

Remember, as the leader, you may want to model some of these answers for your group by sharing from your own experience.

ASK:

» As you watched the video, what impacted you the most? Explain.

» What have been some of your fears of fully trusting Jesus?

» What have been some of the "costs" you've already paid to walk this journey in The Landing?

» What have you "gained" by paying these costs?

» How could reading your Bible and praying help keep you focused on following Jesus? Have you found a time of day that works for you to connect with God in this way?

» How could learning more about God help you trust him more?

» How could trusting God help you follow him more closely?

At the end of this discussion, the leader should close in prayer, thanking God for his grace.

Don't forget to remind your students to spend time with their journals this week, reflecting on what God is teaching them during this journey.

Close by reading the Serenity Prayer together (available on p. 3 of their Student Journal). Keep in mind, some teenagers may not want to read aloud with the rest of the group. That's OK; encourage them to focus on the words being shared.

God, grant me the serenity
to accept the things I cannot change,
the courage to change the things I can,
and the wisdom to know the difference.
Living one day at a time,
enjoying one moment at a time;
Accepting hardship as a pathway to peace;
Taking, as Jesus did,
this sinful world as it is;
Not as I would have it;
Trusting that you will make all things right
If I surrender to your will; So that I
may be reasonably happy in this life
and supremely happy with you forever
in the next. AMEN.

- Reinhold Niebuhr

Serve refreshments of some kind so kids and leaders can hang out and connect. Consider having some healthy options for those who may use food as a way of coping. A ping-pong table, foosball table, or even a few board games will give teenagers an excuse to connect.